The
MARK
of a
MAN

Also by Elisabeth Elliot

Through Gates of Splendor
Shadow of the Almighty
Let Me Be a Woman
A Chance to Die
Discipline: The Glad Surrender
God's Guidance
The Shaping of a Christian Family
Keep a Quiet Heart
The Mark of a Man
Faith That Does Not Falter
Passion and Purity
Quest for Love
Be Still My Soul
The Journals of Jim Elliot
The Music of His Promises
No Graven Image
The Path of Loneliness
Secure in the Everlasting Arms

The MARK of a MAN

Following Christ's Example of Masculinity

ELISABETH ELLIOT

© 1981 by Elisabeth Elliot

Published by Revell
a division of Baker Publishing Group
P.O. Box 6287, Grand Rapids, MI 49516-6287
www.revellbooks.com

New paperback edition published 2006

Printed in the United States of America

Library of Congress Cataloging-in-Publication Data
Elliot, Elisabeth.
    The mark of a man : following Christ's example of masculinity / Elisabeth Elliott. — New pbk. ed.
      p.   cm.
    Includes bibliographical references.
    ISBN 10: 0-8007-3132-8 (pbk.)
    ISBN 978-0-8007-3132-8 (pbk.)
    1. Men (Christian theology) 2. Women—Religious aspects—Christianity.
I. Title.
BT701.3.E45 2006
248.8′42—dc22   2006029437

Scripture marked RSV is taken from the Revised Standard Version of the Bible, copyright 1952 [2nd edition, 1971] by the Division of Christian Education of the National Council of the Churches of Christ in the United States of America. Used by permission. All rights reserved.

Scripture marked NEB is taken from *The New English Bible*. Copyright © 1961 and 1970 by The Delegates of Oxford University Press and The Syndics of the Cambridge University Press. Reprinted by permission.

Scripture marked PHILLIPS is taken from The New Testament in Modern English, revised edition—J. B. Phillips, translator. © J. B. Phillips 1958, 1960, 1972. Used by permission of Macmillan Publishing Co., Inc.

Scripture marked YOUNG CHURCHES are from LETTERS TO YOUNG CHURCHES by J. B. Phillips. Copyright © 1968 by J. B. Phillips. Used by permission.

Quotations from "I'm an Ordinary Man," © 1956 by Alan J. Lerner & Frederick Loewe Chappell & Co., Inc., owner of publication and allied rights throughout the world. International Copyright Secured. ALL RIGHTS RESERVED. Used by permission.

11 12 13 14 15 16   9 8 7 6 5 4

In this book, Elisabeth Elliot brings into focus the separate functions that God assigned to Adam and Eve, which show that the sexes are "gloriously and radically unequal." Written as personal advice to her nephew Pete, her convictions on manliness will help you to see the glory and purpose of true masculinity—and reassure you as you shape your own Christian sexual identity.

Elisabeth Elliot is one of the most loved and respected Christian communicators of our day and is the author of more than twenty books, including *The Journals of Jim Elliot, Through Gates of Splendor, Shadow of the Almighty, The Path of Loneliness, Passion and Purity,* and *A Path through Suffering.*

After eleven years of missionary work in Ecuador, South America, she returned to the United States and continued writing and speaking. Elliot was adjunct professor at Gordon-Conwell Seminary for four years and writer-in-residence at Gordon College for another four years. She and her husband, Lars Gren, live in Magnolia, Massachusetts.

For a complete list of other books and resources from Elisabeth Elliot, visit her website at www.elisabethelliot.org

For Peter Henry deVries

Contents

Introduction

You would be surprised, Pete, at how often you are in my thoughts. And as often as you are in my thoughts, you are in my prayers—you and my other two highly marriageable nephews, Gene and Steve. I pray that God will make you real men and give you for wives—if He wants you to marry—real women.

You are in my thoughts on this dark, winter afternoon. The sea, on which I look out through the window near my typewriter, is battleship gray, running in long swells before a northeast wind. Three little coots ride the swells, vanishing altogether beneath the surface, from time to time, only to pop up again, like corks. The waves churn and foam and slap against the great rocks below the bluff, praising God. "Let them praise the name of the Lord! For he commanded and they were created. And he established them for ever and ever; he fixed their bounds which cannot be passed. Praise the Lord . . . you sea monster and all deeps."

It was just over a week ago that you drove Lars and me to the airport, in the little black car that needs new seats so badly—the car that gave you what you called a Saab story when you first bought it, thinking you were getting

11

a bargain. I remember your troubles that school year—just the sort of troubles one would expect a young man to have: your car, your grades at the university, your girl friend(s!). And, when you called to ask advice, I said, "You know what I'm going to say, don't you, Pete?"

"Yup. that's why I called. I needed to hear it again."

So we talked about learning to know God. Faith has to be exercised in the midst of ordinary, down-to-earth living. Ordinary living includes trouble. When things are going as we would like, faith doesn't often seem necessary. It's when things get messed up that we look around for answers or for help. Where, exactly would you expect the tests for a young man's faith to come, if not in the three areas where you were having trouble?

"Right!" you said.

Then there was the question about participating in a campus Christian group. Not many of us are much good at being Christians all by ourselves—we're supposed to be a flock or a body. We've got to have help: somebody to study the Bible with, somebody to pray with, somebody to lift us up when we're down. You promised to look for a Christian friend.

Of course my prayers were intensified for you after each phone call or letter.

Last week I thought of you again, at a student convention where I was speaking on—among other things—the married woman on the mission field. I was surprised to find in my audience, besides married women, several hundred men and single women. I realized how badly things have gotten twisted in the past decade or so, when—apropos of my thesis that there *is* a difference between men and women, that they're not interchangeable—I called for a show of hands of the men who would like to be asked for a date. I was quite unprepared for the response. Hundreds of hands went up. I should have asked then to see the hands of those who would *not* want to be asked (I wonder if there would have been any), but I was too startled and confused. When I suggested that we post a sign-up sheet at the back of the auditorium, the clapping, cheering, and shrieking (loudest, I suppose, from the single women) was tumultuous. Everybody but me was amused. Children of their time, so accustomed to hearing about *equality* and *rights* and *personhood*, they no longer know what the difference is between the sexes. They even wonder whether it is legitimate to notice any difference or whether it might not be better to pretend there is none.

Well, Pete, there is one.

"Come off it!" I hear you saying, "Think I don't know?"

Of course you know. Everybody knows. The biological difference is—so far, at least—an undeniable datum. There is a certain "unbudgeableness" about simple facts. They won't go away. But science is working hard to change all that. God help us if it succeeds!

But in this era of ERA we've been trying our best to erase, ignore, overcome, or at least smudge the physical facts. Sometimes we hope that if we become truly civilized and "freed up," we'll be above all that and that perhaps, if we get terribly "spiritual," we'll manage to transcend it. The transcendence, however, is not that of real Christian vision at all, but rather of a thoroughly worldly compulsion to rearrange things to fit our humanism. Feminists are busy rewriting all of history, psychology, mythology, sociology, and even theology to suit the spirit of the age, and, if you dare say, "Hey, wait a second!" you know what you'll be called.

There *is* a difference besides the biological one.

13

"You mean all those tired old stereotypes: Men are supposed to do this; women are supposed to do that? Nothing but conditioning! Knee-jerk stuff!"

I've heard that answer, too. Rosemary Radford Reuther, professor of historical theology, in *From Machismo to Mutuality*, speaks of "exposing" masculinity and femininity as "social ideologies." Alas. Christians have lost their bearings when they accept a label like that.

No, Pete. I'm not talking about biology or stereotypes or social ideologies. I'm talking about what sexuality (masculinity and femininity) *means*. Ever stop to wonder if the physiology means anything?

I'm asking you to stop and wonder. There is a great deal more here than meets the eye. There is more than can be explained by custom or culture.

There is a mystery. It's this mystery that I wanted to write about for you. You are a man, Pete, and I know it when I see you. I thank God for your manliness.

I have to catch my breath sometimes, too, remembering the little boy I knew such a short time ago. You hated carrots. But you were obedient, and, if your mother said, "Eat your carrots!" you stuffed them into your mouth. They didn't always get much farther, as we found one day in Quito, Ecuador. Your family and I had been invited to a missionary's home for lunch. You were about four, I think, and took a nap in the missionary's bedroom while we chatted after the meal. On the way home, an hour or so later, you mumbled, "Do I have to finish these carrots?" They were still stashed away in your fat little cheek.

I have a photograph of you and your cousin Valerie chasing pigeons on the Atlantic City boardwalk. It calls up memories of how she would tiptoe ever so delicately, trying to get as close as she could, and you would clump heavily in your tiny Buster Brown shoes and be so disappointed when the pigeons flew off with a whoosh.

You grew up in a few days, it seemed. You lived in the Philippines, where I visited you only once. There you were at the Puerto Princesa airport, which wasn't much more than a lemonade stand, waving a huge banner, WELCOME, AUNT BETTY AND UNCLE ADD! You were about thirteen, I think, but knew how to maneuver a motorboat, water-ski, skindive, run a diesel generator, man a shortwave radio, and beautifully play a violin.

You've added many skills to the list in the years that have intervened. You installed a fluorescent light for me in the kitchen during one Christmas vacation. You've learned to ski and ride horses, and you have a master's degree in concert violin.

The world cries for men who are strong: strong in conviction, strong to lead, to stand, to suffer. I pray that you will be that kind of man, Pete, glad that God made you a man, glad to shoulder the burden of manliness in a time when to do so will often bring contempt. I say to you what Paul said in his letter to the Ephesian Christians:

> Live life, then, with a due sense of responsibility, not as men who do not know the meaning and purpose of life but as those who do. Make the best use of your time, despite all the difficulties of these days. Don't be vague but firmly grasp what you know to be the will of the Lord.

This is a book about the things that mark such men. I trust you will find it sufficiently well documented to prove that it is not simply an interesting or merely quaint point of view, but, in fact, truth that saves.

1

The Way Things Are

Some months ago a scientist named Freeman Dyson described, in a magazine article, some early experiences in the laboratory. He was delighted to be turned loose with crystals and magnets and prisms and spectroscopes to work through some famous old experiments, knowing beforehand how things were supposed to behave. It seemed like a miracle to him when he measured the electric voltage produced by light of various colors falling on a metal surface and found Einstein's law of the photoelectric effect to be really true. But it was in the Millikan oil-drop experiment that he had a revelation. Robert Millikan, a physicist at the University of Chicago, was the one who first measured the electric charge of individual electrons. He made a mist of tiny drops of oil and watched them float around under his microscope while he pulled and pushed them with strong electric fields. Dyson, following Millikan's rules, had gotten the drops floating nicely when he grabbed the wrong knob to adjust the electric field. They found him stretched out on the floor.

This brief and nearly fatal exposure to an immutable law revealed to him what Einstein had meant when he said, "The eternal mystery of the world is its comprehensibility." Dyson realized that his most elaborate and sophisticated calculations about how an electron *ought* to behave would do nothing more than show how it *would* behave, regardless of whether or not he ever bothered calculating its actions. The electrons in the oil drop knew exactly what they were supposed to do and did it—to his peril, when he took hold of the wrong knob.

We're living in a dangerous time. People are tampering with God's arrangements, grabbing the wrong knobs. The results are not always so dramatic and so instantaneous as they were for Dyson, but they are equally inexorable: Sow the wind; reap the whirlwind.

During the past few months I have been in close touch with several married couples who are in deep difficulty because, I believe, they have been infected with the theory that masculinity and femininity are not very important. They have "tampered with the wrong knobs," so to speak, by denying God-given gifts, trying to make husband and wife "equal" and/or interchangeable. Rhetoric about liberation and mutual submission and egalitarianism sound harmless enough, even enlightened; but it is perilous in the extreme, and people are ending up "on the floor," as it were. There *is*, in fact, an arrangement for men and women, just as surely as there is one for electrons. No matter who's paying attention, no matter how carefully or carelessly the scientist in the laboratory may conduct his experiments, the electrons are bound to do certain things. They're bound to do them because they were made to do them. This is the way things are.

Einstein saw the world as "comprehensible"—that is, he recognized its design and predictability, which were, in themselves, its very mystery. Shall we who acknowledge the world's Creator deny that most tremendous of human mysteries: the design for sexuality? Shall we focus instead on something attenuated and poor, something legally or (worse!) sociologically defined?

2

Equal in Being Created

Many men, I find as I travel around, are not especially interested in the questions raised by the "liberation" movements. To be honest, neither was I. The whole business bored me, but, because I happen to be a fairly visible and vocal woman, I was often pressed for a response. Consequently I had to do some homework and find out what was really at issue. The more I understood, the more uneasy I became. *Appalled* would be a more accurate word. I began to see that there are some truly demonic implications in the philosophy behind what is popularly called liberation and that terms have been preempted and given meanings that are often nearly—and sometimes diametrically—opposite to those we have understood in the past. *Salvation* has come to mean "self-fulfillment" or "self-expression"; *freedom* means "release from responsibility"; and *sin* seems to mean little more than "a personal problem of adjustment." This makes it almost impossible for people even to "hear" what God says. Every word that proceeds out of his mouth is redefined, qualified, adjusted to make it acceptable to a secular mind-set. I am acutely aware of this when there is a question-and-answer period following one of my talks. Even when I particularly ask that people try to hold their objections in abeyance long enough to ponder honestly what a certain scriptural principle really *does* mean, the first question is often, "But surely it *doesn't* mean . . . ?" or, "But don't you think that's a matter of semantics?" or, "You can carry that idea to an extreme." What I've just suggested has gone in one ear and out the other. The questioner has not paused for five seconds to ask, "What is *God* saying to *me*?" He is deeply conditioned to accommodate the absolutes to a philosophy of relativism, existentialism, or—to use a word more acceptable to some Christians now—*contextualization*.

What has been called the women's issue is most emphatically men's. It is to you that I write, Pete—you and all the rest of them—earnestly asking that you think, and that you think theologically, about what is really taking place. Responsibility before God lies with all of us, of course—with women as well as with men—but I believe it lies most heavily with you men; and, if you're a conscientious reader, I think you will see why.

Among the words that have subtly changed in meaning is *equality*. This is a confusing one, unless you know precisely what *quality* it refers to. When the Constitution declares that "all men are created equal," it is not referring to intelligence, good looks, good humor, height, weight, or income. It is talking about certain rights, "inalienable" in that they cannot be taken away. They are nothing that one

21

man can give to another. All men and women, it is said, are "endowed by their Creator" with these rights. What are they exactly? "Life, liberty, and the pursuit of happiness." Current talk of "equal rights" covers so many diverse areas that it has caused us to forget which ones the Constitution was trying to guarantee. We've forgotten, too, it seems, that a Creator was mentioned. It's reasonable to assume that if there was a Creator who endowed us, He had a clear purpose in mind.

It's in the Bible that we find out about this Creator. The book starts with the story of the making of heavens and earth; light and darkness; firmament and waters; earth and seas; sun, moon, and stars; plants and animals; men and women. It's a fascinating list of opposites. Reading that list, one would hardly think of the word *equal*. In fact one can only think of distinctions and inequalities.

But our subject is men and women. Men and women, we are being reminded with tiresome regularity, are "equal."

Well, yes, but how? Does it mean equally bright, beautiful, funny, tall, fat, or wealthy? Rubbish! Does it mean "interchangeable"? Surely not. Let's get down to particulars and study the Book that tells us who made them and how and why. If they are not interchangeable, if there are significant differences, we need to see them clearly before men can really be men or women by women.

All we know from the first chapter of Genesis about the man and woman God made would indicate that, apart from the interesting details of sexual differentiation, which gets only passing mention ("Male and female he created them"), they were created equal, with regard to certain particulars.

The first of these is that they were both *created*. We could say, then, that they are equal in having been made. In this sense they were equal also to light and darkness, to sun and stars, to earth and firmament, even to electrons. They were made by Somebody. Theories of beginning, other than the biblical one, require a much more daring act of faith than this. We'll settle for this one.

3

Equal in Image

The next thing in which it's legitimate to speak of the man and the woman being equal sets them apart immediately from all that was created before. Man was made in the image of God. When I say *man*, I'm sure you understand, Pete, that it's a generic word. It applies to both you men and us women, notwithstanding the protests of those who haven't yet got the etymology straight.

"So God created man in his own image." That's a plain enough statement, isn't it? But, just in case it wasn't plain enough, the next phrase restates it: "in the image of God he created him." It's as though God says, "Got that now?"

Yes. We're made in the image of God. I believe that. But I thought God was *spirit*. How can he be represented by a human image? Spirit has no body. Yet the Bible speaks of God's eye, God's hand, God's arm—anthropomorphic terms, we are told, but that's only a label. It doesn't explain a thing. The Bible does not explain the how or the why of our being made in God's image. It simply tells us we are.

It tells us, too, that it took two different modalities to represent this divine image. It took male and female. Why? Is God a sexual being? Wouldn't a sexless, or perhaps a single-celled being have been a more appropriate image? What can male and female possibly have to do with the image of the almighty and eternal God?

Would you like to know the answer, Pete? So would I. But it's not spelled out. It's a mystery. In the very first chapter of the first book in the Bible we touch on the mystery of sexuality. It's one of the conditions of being human. If you're going to be human, you're going to be sexual. You must be either a man or a woman. And *as* a man or a woman you represent the *imago dei*. It is this, the "image of God" that marks man off from all other animals. The Jerusalem Bible says "it involves a general similarity of nature: intellect, will, authority—man is a person. It paves the way for a higher revelation: man's share in the divine nature by virtue of grace."

Human life, then, is fraught with meaning, with transcendence. It is not empty. It is not trivial. It is not mere mechanics.

4

Equal in Moral Responsibility

Besides in their being made by God and in the image of God, men and women can be said to be equal in being placed under moral responsibility. God gave them a command for which both were responsible and which neither could fulfill without the other: Be fruitful and multiply. It takes two to tango. It takes the sexual distinction to make it work: two creatures amazingly alike and wondrously different.

Where there is a command given to human beings, there is a choice—a moral choice. To be made in God's image entails the power to choose, which necessitates a will. Both the man and the woman were endowed with this power. They were free moral agents who were at liberty to obey or to disobey.

Knowing ahead of time the mess they would get into because of this freedom, why did God allow it? It's another deep mystery, but one thing can be said with certainty: God wanted us to choose to love Him. Our freedom to choose that would have been meaningless if we had not also been free not to love Him. The freedom to obey depends on the freedom to disobey.

Adam and Eve did their part, so far as we can tell, to obey the commandments of the first chapter: Be fruitful and increase; fill the earth and subdue it; rule over the fish in the sea, the birds of heaven, and every living thing that moves upon the earth.

It was the commandment of the second chapter that was disobeyed; but more of that later. If all we knew about men and women was what is contained in the first chapter of Genesis, it would be quite accurate to describe them as equal, with the single exception of sexual differentiation.

Those who call themselves feminists—whether "biblical" ones or otherwise—seem to have one belief in common, and only one that I have been able to extract from their arguments: They agree that there is no difference between men and women, apart from the physiological one. It is on this level and this level alone that they recognize men and women as functionally noninterchangeable. Failing to see the physiological as representative of anything higher, they fail altogether to define any theological noninterchangeability. Given this premise, even "biblical" feminists would find nothing to quarrel about in Genesis 1, and, in fact, we could all quite happily be "feminists." Except that of course the term would never have come into being; masculinity and femininity would not have been thought of, and nobody would be trying to prove a thing. It's when we get into Genesis 2 that the division takes on far greater dimensions than physiology.

It is worth noting here—it is worth emphasizing—that those who do trivialize the biological distinction (the feminists, for example, and homosexuals as well) are those who generally recognize no other. It would seem that unless we see *through* and *beyond* the physical, we shall not even see the physical as we ought to see it: as the very vehicle for the glory of God.

The pressure of the world is always heavy, Pete. At present the pressure of secularism and humanism is heavier than ever before. It is these philosophies that have affected the church's thinking about sexuality. Check out the *Humanist Manifesto* (I and II—drawn up in 1933 and 1973) if you want to see exactly what we're up against. Humanists regard the universe as "self-existing and not created," a belief in the supernatural as "either meaningless or irrelevant to the question of . . . the fulfillment of the human race. . . . We begin with humans, not with God. . . . We can discover no divine purpose or providence for the human species. . . . Moral values derive their source from human experience, needing no theological sanction." Humanism is, in fact, frankly called a "religion"! Christians too often are ignorant of where the battle lines are drawn and consequently uncritically accept the terms as defined by the opposition.

5

The Inequalities

We are so accustomed to thinking of justice in terms of equality that we forget the very obvious inequalities with which we have been endowed by our Creator. Perhaps it would be safer to label them *distinctions* rather than *inequalities*, since the latter term nowadays often seems to imply a judgment of worth. Among the divine distinctions are race, sex, color, and IQ. People have been labeled *racist* or *sexist* for valuing one race or sex more highly than another or, it seems at times, for noticing them at all. It's hard to get at just what the labels mean.

Recently we stayed in a hotel where there was a convention of teachers of black children. No one objects to an organization like that. Nobody calls them racist. But, if the convention had been of teachers of white children, somebody might have.

Your uncle Tom recently heard a woman complain that the office where she worked was "very sexist."

"You mean men are being discriminated against?" he queried. She was speechless for a few seconds. She hadn't considered that possibility.

Teachers hesitate to single out the brilliant child and reward him according to his achievements. It might be seen as a put-down of those of lesser gifts. Underachievers, on the other hand, are granted special treatment. The giving of grades is regarded by some educators as undemocratic or even elitist and perhaps dangerously damaging to the ego—the dull ones being those whose egos require careful handling. The ego of the child who ought to have gotten a gold star, but didn't, isn't supposed to be vulnerable.

Concern for the rights of criminals has intensified to the point where they are given ever more preferential treatment in courts and even sometimes in prisons. It appears at times that public sympathy is on their side, rather than on the victims'.

Virginia Mollenkott and Letha Scanzoni have written a book called *Is the Homosexual My Neighbor?* in which they propose what they call a "covenantal" homosexual relationship, a "same-sex union" that they claim does not break the "cohumanity of creation." Homosexuals, they tell us, may then relate to the *other* sex "in non-genital ways."

None of this should surprise us, until we learn that these women consider themselves "biblical feminists," and Mollenkott, at least, has also called herself a Christian humanist. Both seem to me contradictions in terms. Their position is certainly feminist, certainly humanist. It is hard to see how it can be feminist and humanist and at the same time biblical and Christian; for it proceeds from a thoroughly secular premise that men and women are different only biologically and raises the question as to whether any social or moral distinction can or ought to be made between the homosexual and the heterosexual. To make any such distinction, in the opinion of Mollenkott and Scanzoni, is at best ignorant, at worst bigoted and sinful. With all due respect for these women as members of the Body of Christ, I find their rearrangement of society not an improvement, but a profound disorientation of God, man, and the world, leading finally to disintegration and chaos.

What concerns us here is the difference between men and women, not the one between heterosexuals and homosexuals; but it is necessary to examine both areas, since feminism has so obscured the fundamental issue. Some feminists would encourage us to take no particular notice either of the difference between men and women or the difference between "gay" and "straight," as though the first difference has no radiance and the second no murkiness. Masculinity and femininity, being elements of the original design, radiate glory. They shine. They are the norms, carrying in themselves something of God's image. Homosexuality, on the other hand, is a deviation from the original design. It obscures the glory of God's image.

Often I meet people who call themselves feminists because they passionately believe in the "equality of the sexes," yet they would balk at the Mollenkott-Scanzoni defense of a homosexual life-style. They have not thought the issue through. It is extremely important to note that once the first premise of feminism is conceded (that sexual difference is merely physiological, rather than theological) it is reasonable to conclude that men and women may express "sexual preference." Where the very nature and meaning

31

of sexuality is lost, it becomes a matter of taste rather than principle.

Mollenkott's conclusion does not at all surprise me. What surprises me is her claim to submission to the authority of Scripture, when that authority is being radically challenged. Where human sexuality is no longer recognized as a symbol, or where that vital symbol has lost its meaning, it can be reasonably argued that equality is what really matters. Where human sexuality is seen as an indispensable element in the image of God and representative of mystery, the notion of equality is entirely out of place.

Confusion of language is a symptom of confusion of thought. Sexual mores are up for grabs because nobody takes moral absolutes seriously anymore. The confusion that results is represented in vocabulary. A perfectly good political term like *equality* is applied to everybody, regardless of whether the context is political or not. Gradually the word comes to mean "worth just as much as," or "deserving," or even simply "human." I have mentioned widely varied categories in which the word has been used. They serve to illustrate how difficult it is to get at what we really mean by it.

I would not for a moment suggest that the difference between men and women is in the same category with the difference between, for example, smart people and dull ones, criminals and law-abiding folks, or homosexuals and heterosexuals. Yet these differences are so often treated uncritically that we need to back up and examine whether they are important, how they are important, and how the word *equality* applies to them. Sexuality is a glorious distinction. I dare to call it even a glorious inequality, so that we may understand how important it is and how utterly noninterchangeable men and women are. If we understand it, we will rejoice in it—rejoice that God thought of it and loaded it with so much meaning. Far from wanting to play it down, we'll want to celebrate it.

6

The Maker of Distinctions

God is a maker of distinctions. We have already noted that the work of creation entailed some sharp contrasts. The earth was at first formless, "and darkness was upon the face of the deep." With a mighty word of command, "Let there be light . . . ," God created light. He separated things (such as light from darkness), and He named them (names like day and night. ". . . And there was evening and there was morning, one day."

Then He separated the waters from the waters, with what He called a firmament; and He called the firmament heaven. That was the second day.

And so on through five separate days of creative activity, God went right on making distinctions. He made dry land and seas, plants and trees. He made two great lights, one to rule the day and the other to rule the night. Then He formed creatures appropriate to the media in which they were to

34

dwell: birds to fly in the air, monsters to swarm in the oceans (just yesterday a 400-pound giant squid was washed up on a beach near here, and it took ten men to "get it together" and haul it away), things that crawl and beasts that walk on dry land. ". . . And God saw that it was good."

He crowned this stupendous labor by bringing forth the most glorious of earthly creatures—man—made in His image and destined to rule over the rest of the earth. But even this creature appeared, like all other animals, in two distinct forms: male and female. The distinction was God's idea. *We* wouldn't have thought of it. Imagine a sexless world. If you're looking for Dullsville, that would be it, wouldn't it? We've had enough hints of what it would be like in the unisex world of blue jeans. When men and women accept the sexual difference and enjoy it, they put color and design and variety into life. When they begin to deny it or to feel that it should somehow be blurred, they take all the color out (except for denim blue—and they are careful to take even some of that out, with Clorox, before the color is acceptable!).

It's hard to tell the men from the women at a college weekend retreat: the down-filled vests, the turtlenecks, the jeans, the waffle-stompers, the hair hanging in the eyes, the backpacks.

"Oh, wow!" some of them would say. "She doesn't *like* us!"

Alas. Another distinction gone by the board. You are smart enough to see, Pete, that I'm not condemning. I'm describing. And if the description fits, kids squirm. I'm only holding up a mirror, saying, "Look at yourselves! What do you see?" If it's monochromatic, it illustrates my point: To equalize is to deprive of glory.

7

Just a Person

After a talk I gave at a church in Boston, a person (I use the word advisedly) came swaggering up to me, hands thrust into jeans' pockets, belligerent jaw thrust forward and working vigorously on a wad of gum.

"You know, I disagree with a lot of the stuff you say."

"Okay. You're allowed to disagree with me. But can you be specific? Tell me two things you disagree with."

"Well, I don't know, I mean, like, you know, I just don't like some of the stuff you say about women."

It wasn't the time to point out the difference between not liking and not agreeing. I find that my students in the seminary often confuse the two. Dislike is a mere matter of taste. Nobody can argue with tastes. Disagreement requires refutation. You've got to be able to show the holes in the logic and present a case that demolishes the other's. But I met her on her own terms.

"Okay. Fine. Tell me what you don't like."

"Well, like, you know, I just don't like to think of myself as, like, you know, as a *woman*." The gum was getting a terrific workout.

"Really? How do you like to think of yourself, then?"

"Just a person. You know?"

Everything about this person testified that she was trying. She was doing her best not to be a woman. But it was a poor show, because, come to think of it, there aren't that many options. There's no such animal as a sexless person. To be a person is to be a man or a woman, so of course she ended up acting like a man—and quite an uncouth man, at that.

My heart went out to her, Pete. You know her type. We've talked about them and agreed that there are thousands who have been sold a bill of goods. She's been made to feel that sexuality is something to be ashamed of—and this in the age of "freedom"! She's actually believed those sometimes-brilliant and always illogical women who tell her that her freedom lies in becoming as indistinguishable from men as possible. Do *their* thing, they seem to be saying; that is, do what men do.

The *Humanist Manifesto*, signed by many of the most outspoken feminist leaders, declares that no form of sexual behavior between consenting adults should be prohibited, nor should "the many varieties of sexual exploration" be considered evil. The use of words such as *ideal, normal, masculinity*, and *femininity* are thought, by many feminists, to be inimical to freedom, for they indicate intolerable attitudes that unduly repress sexual conduct. In other words, one of the goals in public-school education is to allow children— even grade-school children—the "freedom to choose" bisexuality, asexuality, homosexuality, or heterosexuality. The

National Organization of Women is determined to achieve what they call "full civil rights for lesbians"; and the Gay Teachers' Alliance is working hard in California to see that sex education in elementary schools includes homosexual education. Referring to the need for homosexual "role models" as teachers, Gloria Steinem said at the International Women's Year convention in Colorado, in 1977, "Children are being deprived of full human talent."

It's no wonder the poor girl in Boston felt apologetic about being a woman. Life would be so much easier, it seemed to her, if we could forget about sex. She didn't know where she belonged. A lot of men don't know where they belong, either, and we're in trouble.

8

The Trouble We're In

A few months ago a hundred and fifty men and women met at Harvard Divinity School for the Second Lesbian and Gay Seminarians' Conference. One Brian McNaught told the story of his water fast, an attempt to get his bishop at least to admit the "*equality* of homosexuals as God's children," if not to ordain them. There's that word again! We would agree that included in the company of God's children are homosexuals as well as all other varieties of sinners—Paul gives quite a list in 1 Corinthians 6: the impure, the idolator, the adulterer, the effeminate, the pervert, the thief, the swindler, the drunkard, the foul-mouthed, the rapacious. "*And such men, remember, were some of you!* But you have cleansed yourselves from all that. . . ." There's the condition. Surely neither McNaught's bishop nor any other good Christian would exclude the homosexual from the priesthood once he had been cleansed and ". . . made whole in spirit . . . justified . . . in the Name of the Lord Jesus and in His very Spirit." But what those seminarians were asking for was acceptance and equality for practicing homosexuals, with or without repentance. They were asking for the erasing of a distinction that is not merely social, but, to the Christian, moral; for sexual activity is rigorously restricted to marriage, according to the Bible. If a person's orientation happens to be toward the same sex, he is, like all others who are not married, bound to celibacy.

Another woman at the same seminarians' conference "filled us with joy," wrote Suzanne Searle, "When she told us that we, better than anyone else, know what is meant by the incarnation of the word, because we live it every day. . . . We, the lesbians and gay men of the church, are fools for Christ. . . . We are a people, a strong people, and a large people. For those who wish to join us, we'll see you this spring in New York."

The arguments adduced to support homosexuality were satirized in a piece in the little ministers' magazine *Monday Morning*. The writer imagines a time in the future when a candidate for ordination will be turned down by presbytery merely because he is an avowed, practicing, proud-as-punch polygamist:

> I can conceive of no more unloving, un-Christian, judgmental action than this. I was declared "morally unfit" to serve as teaching elder in the United Presbyterian Church, USA. . . . It is about time that we, the most neglected, oppressed, misunderstood, unloved minority in this unjust society achieve full status and equal rights . . . I am deeply crushed by this harsh condemnation by the Body of Christ.
>
> As if three or even four consenting adults could not have a meaningful, stable, and loving relationship! Polygamy is *not* promiscuity! . . . As for the oft-quoted Pauline saying,

"be the husband of one wife," 1 Timothy 3:2, we know of *his* problems dealing with sexual preference. At any rate, most modern scholars agree that he probably was reacting to a particular abuse in a particular church and not to all Christians in all situations.

The time has come for polygamists to come out of the closest and demand our rights. The church should be leading this new civil rights thrust.

The writer identified himself as a monogamist in good standing with his presbytery. We can laugh at his satire— except that its actual fulfillment is already in view. . . . Only a month after writing that last sentence, I learned that there is an organization that, while calling itself Christian, seriously advocates incest as a valid "Christian alternative." *Time* also printed an article called "The Last Taboo," in which it was reported that incest is no longer considered by many to be either criminal or abnormal.

Seabury Press, the official publishing house of the Episcopal Church, has recently produced a book called *The Sex Atlas*, in which author Erwin J. Haeberle denies any need for "social interference in the case of sexual contact between humans and animals." Child molestation and incest "should no longer be called crimes, unless they involve unwilling children." We are to assume, I suppose, that in the illustration of a man copulating with a water buffalo the animal was "willing."

It is only a matter of time until books by those who go by the name of evangelical appear under such titles as *Is the Pederast . . .* or *Is the Polygamist My Neighbor?* The answer, of course is *yes*. My neighbor needs me as the victim of thieves needed the Samaritan in the story Jesus told. The Samaritan did not, like the priest, close his eyes to the man's condition and pass by on the other side, but saw him as one in need of rescue. So the Christian looks upon all men and women. They need to be saved. They don't need to be told "I'm O.K., and you're O.K.!" The appropriate remedy (like oil and wine in the story) has to be applied. "The blood of Jesus Christ . . . cleanseth us from all sin."

But, if the original distinction is lost—the vital one between men and women—we end up recognizing no distinctions in sexual conduct. It is the logical conclusion. If sex has no transcendent meaning, what difference does it make whom you go to bed with? You can be promiscuous, homosexual, incestuous, bestial, or otherwise perverted. The only lasting sanctions against such behavior are based on the divine man-woman order.

9

A Local Vertical

Several years ago I read a fascinating account of five men who spent eighty days in a space capsule. What they had to endure because of the phenomenon of weightlessness opened my eyes to how fundamentally necessary it is for us mortals to know which end is up. The men had no "local vertical," that is, no point of reference apart from their own heads and feet, because the capsule they were in was a cylinder which was, so far as they were concerned, "lying on its side." They did not walk, they floated. They had to shove themselves sideways off a wall and hope they would glide to wherever they intended to go. Since gravity did not operate, it was impossible to take a bath, because water didn't stay in a tub. They couldn't take a shower, because water didn't fall. It floated in globes, because of surface tension; or, if it happened to touch anything, formed hemispheres, because of cohesion with a flat surface. Pills wouldn't fall out of a bottle; food would not stay on forks; the pages of books fanned open like flowers; one man's shaggy hair always looked like a "furious sandstorm"; and the men's faces puffed up because gravity did not pull blood to the feet. If a man wanted to shave, he had to be very nimble when he opened his shaving kit, because everything drifted out, and he found himself frantically trying to pluck his razor and shaving cream from mid air. When one man tried to turn a screw with a screwdriver, the screw turned him. He found his entire body revolving, while the screw didn't budge.

Nothing worked the way it was supposed to. Even the sun came up sixteen times and set sixteen times in twenty-four hours.

When asked about the extreme disorientation they had experienced during those interminable weeks, one man said, "Boy, it's so lousy I don't even want to talk about it. You like things to be orderly."

Proverbs 19:10 says, "A fool at the helm is out of place, how much worse a slave in command of men of rank!"

The book of Isaiah describes the Day of the Lord of Hosts, a terrible time when, because of the judgment of God, disorder will reign. Mighty men, soldiers, judges, prophets, diviners, elders, captains, men of rank, counselors will be taken away, and He will make boys their princes, ". . . and babes shall rule over them. . . . My people—children are their oppressors, and women rule over them. O my people, your leaders mislead you, and confuse the course of your paths."

Chaos. But doesn't it sound familiar? Everything upside down. Those who rightly hold authority divested of it, those who properly are subject are now in charge. We need a local vertical, a point of reference other than our own heads and feet—one which does not shift.

10

The Ancient Story

Myths are stories that tell how things got started. We usually think of the word *mystical* as a synonym for *fictitious*, but myths may or may not be historical accounts. If I were to say that the Genesis account of the creation and fall of man were myths, some readers would be relieved, others alarmed. I do say that they are; not in the sense that they are tales springing from some primeval imagination, but that they are stories—*true* ones—about how things began; and as such they testify to the deepest consciousness in us of what it means to be human. There is in all of us an awareness that humanness is radically distinct from animalness; that being men or women is somehow far more important than a mere matter of not having fur, feathers, or fins, and that as rational creatures, we are also responsible creatures. This awareness is explained by the creation story, which, like the rest of the Bible, is inspired by God. We get our bearings from it and find our local vertical.

We have seen what the first chapter in the Bible says about how things began. The second chapter in the Bible tells the story of creation in greater detail. We find there that it was the man who was made first.

I visited a class in Texas of what are called exceptional children, which in this case meant those with learning disabilities. The teacher had warned me that they were usually very shy when strangers were present, but she promised to do her best to get them to talk to me. She knew I'd love that.

"Tell the lady," she said to the class, "what God made the first man out of."

"Dirt!" shouted out one small boy.

"Fine. And what did He do next?"

"He blowed sense into 'im!" shouted another.

A vivid translation. "The Lord God formed man of dust from the ground, and breathed into his nostrils the breath of life. . . ."

We might conclude, from all we've learned so far about the two sexes, that they are "equal," except in the one (minor?) detail of standard procreative equipment. That had to be differentiated, we can understand, but only for function. It had no other importance.

Hadn't it? Better give some attention to the details in that second chapter. They let us in on some facts that suggest a far deeper mystery in this business of sexuality than might have met the eye in the first chapter. These facts point to what I call the vital equalities.

Everything God made struck Him as good or very good, until He came to one thing. He had made the man in His image, "blowed sense into 'im," put him in a garden and

46

given him work to do, provided him with food, instructed him about the one danger that existed, and then "noticed," if we may use the word, one thing that was not good. It was not a good thing for the man to be alone. He needed a helper designed to fit. (And please, Pete, not a *helpmate*! That's a corruption of two perfectly good old words: *help* and *meet*, which means "suited" or "especially appropriate.") Then "out of the ground," the Lord formed all the animals and birds (the chronology in this chapter is slightly different from that of the first, but there are various scholarly explanations of this, which you can look up if you want to) and brought them to the man "to see what he would call them." I love picturing God presenting them, one by one, waiting eagerly while Adam thought up a name. Whatever he thought up was all right with God. But in the whole zoo, from aardvarks to zebras, there wasn't a help anywhere that was really *meet*. There was nothing that would *fit* the specifications.

So of course God made one. He put Adam to sleep and took a rib out of his side, sutured him up again, and made the borrowed bone into a woman.

Then there's another picture I love to ponder: the presentation. God brought this brand-new creature to Adam, and Adam recognized her at once as his own. The story is very short here, much too short for my taste. I would love to have had a detailed description of exactly what they both looked like, how Eve approached Adam, how he looked at her, what he was thinking, and whether God said anything by way of introduction. But we know all we need to know. Adam named her. He called her "woman"—*ishshah*, in Hebrew, because she was taken of out of man, *ish*.

In that little story, which takes up only seventeen verses, men and women can find their local vertical. Four extremely important events illuminate where woman stands in relation to man. I see, in them, who I am as a woman, who you are as a man.

1. She was made *for* the man. According to specifications, she was divinely designed to fit his needs exactly—an adapter, a responder.
2. She was made *from* the man, quite literally, constructed out of one of his own bones. He was her reason for being, her *source*, which is one of the root meanings of the New Testament word for "head." If you miss the point in Genesis 2, you can pick it up in 1 Corinthians 11: "For man was not made from woman, but woman from man. Neither was man created for woman, but woman for man."

   "Oh, well," people have said to me, "you're just interpreting things your way. There are lots of other interpretations." Are there? Give three examples.
3. She was brought *to* the man. God made a present of Eve to Adam, not of Adam to Eve. She was his.
4. She was named *by* the man. The Old Testament authority to name was of immense importance. It signified the acceptance of responsibility. He was taking charge.

That's the ancient story.

11

Too Wonderful for Solomon

The ancient story is followed by a *therefore*. The simple facts are packed with significance. The creation of this man and this woman in this manner and the bringing them together is the divine institution of marriage. The implications of that institution are hinted at in the sentence that immediately follows the story: "Therefore a man leaves his father and mother [renunciation] and cleaves to his wife, [the establishment of a new and permanent social unit] and they become one flesh [total and indissoluble intimacy]."

The separation of all males and females was created in order that a particular male and female might be united. This union required another separation, this time from parents. The man and woman are then no longer two, but "one flesh," as Jesus told the Pharisees. It is *God* who has joined them.

It's a serious business, Pete. Sometimes you hear people say that sex is "a perfectly natural function," meaning that it is no different or no more important than eating and drinking. They're dead wrong. People throughout history have known that a whole lot more is at stake here than in other "natural functions." That's why sex has always been surrounded with ceremony and sanctions and rules and taboos and secrecy.

I found that Auca Indians spoke very often and very freely about all bodily functions except sex. They did talk about sex, too, but in a different way. They did not refer to their own activities. They would make jokes about the surmised sex life of everybody else—laughing themselves sick over so-and-so's imagined congress with a tree toad or a toucan, but not inquiring seriously into what actually went on or giving away any of their own tricks.

Anybody who contemplates sexuality for as much as five minutes knows that he is up against a mystery. Who can understand all that is implied in that renunciation, that new establishment, that intimacy? Who can explain the dynamics between a man and a woman? Solomon, the wisest man who ever lived, confessed himself beaten:

> Three things are too wonderful for me;
> four I do not understand:
> the way of an eagle in the sky,
> the way of a serpent on a rock,
> the way of a ship on the high seas,
> and the way of a man with a maiden.

The apostle Paul, too, admitted that there was much more in marriage than he could fathom. More of his views later.

Some feminists treat marriage as though it were a diabolical plot. "We must reform and abolish the institution of legal marriage," Gloria Steinem said. The Declaration of Feminism, drawn up in Minneapolis, in 1972, stated, "Marriage has existed for the benefit of men. The end of the institution of marriage is a necessary condition for the liberation of women. We must work to destroy it."

In a recent television interview, Germaine Greer described what she called her "outlaw kind of sex life," and went on to say, "Marriage should be a socioeconomic contract. Marrying someone you're in love with is crazy stuff." When Dick Cavett asked whether she had anything good to say about marriage, her answer was, "Nope." What about God? She left no doubt about where she stood on that subject. "I don't believe in God. If there is a God, I don't like Him—I mean, the idea. He and I will be on opposite sides. I'll be in guerrilla warfare. If He's up there, what the hell is He doing?"

Clearly such women are adrift. Yet other women follow them, blindly hoping that what they are offering is freedom and fulfillment. The awful truth is that what they offer is bondage and destruction; for they would strip us all—men and women alike—of all mystery and, indeed, of our very humanity. You can't be human and not be a sexual creature. You can't be human and not be made in the image of God. You can't be human and not be a bearer of mystery. You can't be man in relation to a woman and not be skirting very close to one of the deepest mysteries of all.

12

Nothing Buttery

The ancient story is not merely a campfire tale: "It was a dark and stormy night. . . ." It has to do with our present existence, with what is universal, with what is mysterious yet undeniably *there*. It is the great clue to the Way Things Are.

The temptation for all of us is to look only at the surface of a thing and say, "It's nothing but so and so," reducing it to a mere object with no "inside story" whatever. This "nothing buttery," as someone has named it, is profanity, pure and simple. I don't mean cussing. I mean treating as meaningless what is actually full of meaning. To take the name of God "in vain"—to use it thoughtlessly—is profanity.

Masculinity and femininity are being treated profanely. I can't pin them down once and for all, or spell out all the ramifications, or dictate the details of how they ought to look in late twentieth-century America. They are, I admit, elusive symbols. The best I can do is to help you shore up your own conviction that there is definitely something there, that your hunches and intuitions and inarticulate consciousness of the importance of a sexual distinction are correct. They may be merely bubbles that rise to the surface, but there wouldn't be any bubbles if there weren't something at the bottom. There's something down there infinitely more important to your human nature and your identity as a man than any legal or social status could possibly be. There was a time when we could accept this as a reality, a fact, a given, although we were usually unconscious of it. It was something to be lived rather than understood. But, with all the wild absurdities that are being dished out nowadays, the time has come to find out if it really is "nothing but" an anatomical detail.

A lot of time is spent talking about divorce, abortion, homosexual "marriage," the ordination of women or homosexuals, the roles of men and women in the church and home. Unfortunately a lot of that time is wasted, because the prior question has never been asked. Try it on your friends sometime, Pete. Ask the prior question, "Is sexuality anything more than biology?" They look keenly at you for a second or two: Where are you coming from, man? "No, I'm serious. Does it *mean* something?" They won't know what you're talking about, although most of them have very firm opinions about everything that touches on the subject. Start mentioning the possibility of mystery and you'll see the jaws slacken and the eyes glaze.

No wonder it seems immaterial whether homes survive or disintegrate, whether you go to bed with males or females, whether husbands lead or wives "wear the pants." Profanity has made us careless. Like the men in the space capsule, we're afloat where laws no longer operate, and we don't know which end is up.

53

13

Masculinity Means Initiation

"God is so masculine," wrote C. S. Lewis, "that all creation is feminine by comparison." The earth has always been seen in the human imagination as female: Mother Earth, Mother Nature. The sun is usually thought of as male, often as a god. For the earth receives, is acted upon, and gives back in fertility what is planted, while the sun receives nothing from earth, but shines in his strength upon her, giving her life. Here we have the ancient and deep human consciousness of maleness and femaleness.

The nature that happens to be outside my window as I write—the Atlantic Ocean—seems anything but feminine today. Although the sun shines dazzlingly on this winter day, there is a great storm far out at sea, the weatherman told us; and consequently the waves are roaring and pounding onto the giant rocks below the house, rushing like steeds with heads lowered and white manes flying, storming into the rocks, rearing and leaping, then exploding into plumes and clouds and columns of spray. As the water is sucked back the foam creams and swirls; a thousand streams cascade down the face of the rock; and there are a few seconds of silence, as though the sea held its breath, before the next rush of cavalry. The power, the thunder, and the aggressiveness are masculine to me. If someone suggests that they are masculine only to me and only because of the usual prejudices, I would refer him to poetry and legend and myth and story. I would refer also to Scripture, naturally. God chose images of strength in nature—one of which is the sea—to represent Himself:

> I . . . will bring up many nations against you, as the sea brings up its waves. They shall destroy the walls of Tyre, and break down her towers; and I will scrape her soil from her, and make her a bare rock.
> . . . mightier than the waves of the sea, the Lord on high is mighty.

Yet even the sea, mighty as it is, is subject. The sea is His, and He made it. It receives its very being, as well as its daily instructions, from the Creator and Sustainer of the world. God is the initiator. This is the distilled essence of masculinity: initiation. All creation responds to His initiating. It is the only thing creation can do.

The principle of initiation is illustrated plainly in the story of Adam and Eve. What are called instinctive notions of masculinity are deeper than stereotypes. Stereotypes have to do with the surface of things. They are fixed and conventional notions of how people are supposed to look and behave.

"Let's get rid of the stereotypes," say the liberators. "Stereotypes lock us in. They're nothing but social conditioning."

I agree. What I disagree with is the belief that masculinity is merely stereotyped. Many of our notions are accurate reflections of *archetypes*—forms of a strongly emotional character, which in some way reflect the internal structure of the world. They are the original models or patterns from which all other things of the same kind are made, a very different thing from social conditioning.

Psychologists sometimes describe belief in God as a father as nothing more than a projection of the stereotyped father. It never seems to occur to them that if two things are alike, one ought to ask whether the first is copied from the second or the second from the first. Why should it not be at least as logical to assume that human fathers are copies of the Original? Those who take the Bible as their rule see God as the archetype. From Him are derived all ideas of what fathers ought to be.

To do away with mere stereotypes because they have become useless or burdensome can be a healthy thing. But when, in the effort to get rid of them, we mistakenly attack what are really archetypes, we are in trouble. Promising to liberate and illuminate, we have lately limited and obscured the truth of our sexual nature.

God is the initiator. The pronouns, the names, and the imagery He chose for Himself are largely masculine. To the man Adam He assigned the position of initiator. I infer this first from the chronological order of creation. Adam was made first, then Eve.

I would not try to argue that this proved Adam's authority over Eve if it were all the evidence we had. Chronological order, in fact, might "prove" that sea monsters had authority over Adam since, according to one of the Genesis accounts, it appears that they were created before he was. But we have a New Testament interpretation which is enlightening. Paul's reason for not putting women in positions of authority over men was based on the order of creation and on the order in which the man and woman sinned.

There are other strong reasons for holding that masculinity means initiation. Before we go on to them, we need to look at what femininity means.

14

Femininity Means Response

Eve was made to order. God saw the shape of Adam's need and designed the woman to fit it exactly in every way. She was to be an adapter. When you're looking for the right woman to marry, Pete, look for one who is prepared to adapt to you. Now don't suppose for a minute that you yourself won't have to budge. When two people live together day and night, for life, both of them need to give and take; and I'll mention more of this later. But if you find a woman who is ready to go where you go and do what you do without brooding about being "her own person," you'll have found a treasure. She will have to be a woman who has submitted herself to God, first of all, because otherwise she'll be listening to the insistent voices around her, telling her that she's got to be independent and autonomous, that she ought not to be "only" somebody's wife or somebody's mother, that she needs to seek fulfillment for herself, and that that can only be found beyond the bounds of home. If, having submitted herself to God, she understands that what He had in mind when He made her was response—in order that both man and woman be fulfilled—she will be at peace with the arrangement.

Her femininity is bound up not only with her having been made for the man, but also in having been made from him. Her very existence depended on his having been there first. But then, there would never have been a second man if there hadn't been a woman. Paul puts this clearly: "Of course, in the sight of God neither 'man' nor 'woman' has any separate existence. For if woman was made originally for man, no man is now born except by a woman, and both man and woman, like everything else, owe their existence to God"—a reiteration of all creation's being "feminine" by comparison.

The important thing for you, as a man, to remember, Pete, is that a woman cannot properly be the responder, unless the man is *properly* the initiator. He must take the lead in order that she may follow, as in a dance. The willingness of each to perform the "steps" that have been choreographed gives the other freedom.

The New Testament word for a woman's position is *hupotasso*, "to place or arrange under, to subordinate, to bring under influence." It is used of the spirits of prophets, subject or subordinated to the prophets; and of the whole of creation, subject to Christ. Jesus as a boy submitted Himself to His parents, and the same root word is used as is used of demons being submissive to the disciples in Christ's name. It is a matter of placement. It does not by any means necessarily imply that one is of lesser worth, any more than

Jesus' being placed in a position "inferior to the angels" suggests that angels are worth more than Jesus. (It was, in fact, His willingness to take that position that resulted in His being given "a name beyond all names.")

A young woman told me that she had been very angry about the idea that she was to be subject to her husband. She thought, in the first place, that the traditional view of women was demeaning. To submit is to admit inferior worth. When she acknowledged the lordship of Christ in her life, the truth finally got through to her that submission to her husband was one of the subheadings of that. She had no trouble placing herself under him, once she had thoroughly placed her life under the authority of Christ.

When a man is tempted to excuse selfishness or authoritarianism or tyranny on the basis of this command to the woman to be subject, the thought of the superstructure—that she is actually submitting to Christ by submitting to him—will surely give him pause and, by the grace of God, will gentle him.

If the husband can look upon his gift of initiation as a privilege, instead of as a right; and if the wife can look upon her gift of response in the same way, instead of as an obligation, both might be surprised to find that Jesus' promise actually comes true for them: The yoke proves to be easy, the burden light.

15

The Design

Another hint as to the meaning of masculinity and femininity is the structural design. Because we, as Christians, see the world not as opaque, but shot through with glory ("charged with the grandeur of God," according to Gerard Manley Hopkins), we take the stuff of the world—all physical matter—as being loaded with meaning. "The heavens declare the glory of God and the firmament showeth His handiwork."

"Since the beginning of the world the invisible attributes of God, e.g. His eternal Power and Divinity, have been plainly discernible through things which He has made and which are commonly seen and known. . . ." He continues, today, to reveal to us spiritual truth through physical things if only we have eyes to see them. "Figures of the true" is what Amy Carmichael of India called them. "Everything means everything," says Thomas Howard in *Chance or the Dance?*

But we don't always see very well. Jesus was up against what I have called profanity: people's failure to see things on more than one level. When He spoke with the woman of Samaria, she understood the water to mean only some sort of magic water He was promising, which would release her forever from the drudgery of carrying it from the well. No, He told her, it was another kind: water of life. When He spoke of bread, the disciples could think only of the usual kind. No, He said, it was the Bread of Life. When He spoke of the temple, the Jews took him to mean the one in Jerusalem, while what He meant was His body. We are "of the earth, earthy," and our spiritual eyes are often clouded. "God likes matter," C. S. Lewis says. So do we, but are not always sure we should. We are easily misled into thinking of it as opposed to spirit, when in fact it is the divinely de-signed vehicle of the spirit—the means through which we perceive if we will only open our eyes to what it means.

The physical body ought to tell us something. Many times, in Scripture, the body (specifically, for example, the tongue, eyes, ears, and hand) is mentioned as significant of spiritual things. Isaiah 50 says, "The Lord God has given me the *tongue* of those who are taught, that I may know how to sustain with a word him that is weary. Morning by morning he wakens, he wakens my *ear* to hear as those who are taught." Psalm 19, ". . . the commandment of the Lord is pure, enlightening the *eyes*." Men are told that they ought to pray everywhere, ". . . lifting holy *hands* without anger or quarreling." The *heart* is seen throughout the Bible as the source of action—that is, the will.

People come with standard equipment. Tongue, eyes, ears, hands, heart are usually provided for both men and women. But there is equipment which is radically differentiated: the reproductive system. Its functions are plain enough. Quite unarguably, they are designed for initiation and reception. Is it unreasonable to probe deeper than the temporal function and recognize that these, too, are signs? May we not infer from them, as well as from creation's order, the meaning of masculinity—initiation; and of femininity—response? That's clue number two.

Number one was the order.

Number two is the design.

16

Divine Imagery

There is yet another hint, and a strong one, that the role of initiator is strictly a masculine one. In His relationship with His people Israel, God called Himself the Bridegroom and Israel the Bride. ". . . as the bridegroom rejoices over the bride, so shall your God rejoice over you." The nation of Israel is compared by Ezekiel to an unwanted child, thrown unwashed and naked into an open field, but found and rescued and reared by the Lord. "When I passed by you again and looked upon you, behold you were at the age for love; and I spread my skirt over you, and covered your nakedness: yea, I plighted my troth to you and entered into a covenant with you, says the Lord God, and you became mine." That's a clear picture of one who finds and cares for and woos and cherishes and "husbands." To *husband* means simply "to take care of." Animal husbandry is the care of animals.

In the New Testament, the imagery is repeated in describing the relationship of Christ to the Church. He is the Bridegroom. We men and women who, by believing, make up His church, are called His bride. We're all, as Lewis says, "feminine by comparison." The bride is synonymous with the holy city in the book of Revelation. John saw the city ". . . coming down out of heaven from God, prepared as a bride adorned for her husband," and he heard a great voice saying ". . . Behold, the dwelling of God is with men. He will dwell with them, and they shall be his people, and God himself will be with them; he will wipe away every tear from their eyes. . . ." That the almighty and eternal God should choose us and make us fit to be His own bride and His dwelling place and then restrict Himself to live with *us* and pay the tenderest attention to our needs—what a description of everlasting love! And what a lesson, Pete, for bridegrooms.

I was asked to be on a panel in Virginia on the subject of the roles of men and women in the church. When I mentioned that the imagery chosen by God the Holy Spirit to represent Himself in Scripture was that of a bridegroom, a minister on the panel protested. "Oh," he said, "I don't think that makes any difference at all, really."

"Do you think God might just as well have chosen to represent Himself as the bride, and the church as the groom?"

"Of course," was his answer. "It's only figurative, anyway."

I always thought figurative speech stood for something. I thought it represented one concept in terms of another that might be analogous to it. I still think so. It was not for nothing that these figures of speech were employed. In fact, it's when you are dealing with things too profound for ordinary language that the language of imagery is used. The figures stand for something very important about God.

It will be objected by some that there are female figures of speech used also in reference to God: Jesus used that of a hen with her chicks, in speaking of His longing to gather Jerusalem "under his wings." "As one whom his mother comforts, so I will comfort you," the Lord says, but this refers to His comforting them *through* Jerusalem. It is Jerusalem in this case, that is like a mother: "Rejoice with her in joy, all you who mourn over her; that you may suck and be satisfied with her consoling breasts. . . ."

There are other verses that might be quoted, but their number is small compared to those that unequivocally represent masculinity. We note, too, that it is the male pronoun that is used exclusively when speaking literally of God.

At a convention (they called it a caucus) of evangelical women, a few years ago, the opening hymn had been emasculated. Instead of singing "Dear Lord and Father of Mankind" they sang "Dear Mother/Father of us all." *Lord* and *mankind* were stricken out as sexist terms. *Father* was acceptable only if preceded by *mother*. This is a deliberate rejection of the inspired revelation of God. It is to say that Jesus' own representation of the Father was faulty and inadequate.

Some argue that Jesus restricted Himself to these "sexist" terms only in order not to unduly offend Jews whose patriarchal orientation precluded their acceptance of anything so revolutionary as the equality of men and women. This is a desperate and spurious argument, to say the least. Jesus never pussyfooted. He said outrageously revolutionary things: "Lose your life and you'll find it," "Love your enemies," "Anyone who looks down on his brother as a lost soul is himself heading straight for the fire of destruction." "You appear like good men on the outside—but inside you are a mass of pretense and wickedness. What miserable frauds you are, you scribes and Pharisees! . . ." Was that language inflammatory? Might it have offended? And what about His tremendous claim "I and the Father are One"? This so infuriated the Jews that they picked up stones to stone Him to death. When Jesus asked for which of the good things He had shown them they intended to stone Him, they said it was not for any of the good things, but for blasphemy, "Because you, who are only a man, are making yourself out to be God."

He did not fear them, their knowledge of the law, their power, or their patriarchal "prejudices." And if the only begotten Son, who is in the bosom of the Father, called Him Father, what sort of pride would it be in us to amend and correct that name?

17

Prejudice or Gift

The refusal to accept things which cannot or ought not to be changed is neurotic. These matters of what men are and what women are have been beautifully thought out and put in place. The sooner and the more wholeheartedly we settle into the places assigned, the greater will be our peace and the more harmonious our world. Resentment about it leads to neurosis and bondage.

Adam and Eve did not, so far as we know, take issue with God about His first commandments to them, but they did take issue with Him in the matter of a certain fruit. God put the man in a garden where he was supposed to do the gardening. He was told he could eat from any tree, except the tree of the knowledge of good and evil, which would kill him. This happened before the woman was created, but later, when she had an encounter with the subtle serpent, who must have been a very appealing creature, he persuaded her that she need not take God too seriously. It's clear that Adam had told her of God's command, because she was able to quote it pretty accurately, making it even a bit stricter—she said that not only were they not supposed to eat it, they were not even supposed to touch it. (That might have been Adam's addendum, of course, if he had by then learned a little about woman's curiosity.) Nonsense, was the gist of the serpent's reply. God was being a bit niggardly, wasn't He, in forbidding them such a trifle? You not only won't die, you'll be able to see what you couldn't see before. You'll be like God! As a matter of fact, Eve began to suspect, it was no trifle God had forbidden. It was huge enjoyment. It was life and fulfillment and happiness that God didn't want them to have. God was a sadist. She would be much better off if she ate the proscribed fruit. She would, in fact, no longer be "only" a woman, or even only human. She'd be divine. She liked the sound of that. It was logical and enticing and spelled bliss.

The story says that she then saw—she had apparently not noticed before, perhaps had not even dared to look—that the tree was good for food, a delight to the eyes, and to be desired to make one wise. So she had a taste. Only a teeny one, I suppose, but enough to prove to her that the serpent knew what he was talking about. It was delicious, and just as he had predicted, nothing bad happened. Things were fine. So she took the initiative, and here things got into an even worse mess. Adam and Eve reversed the roles. She offered the fruit to Adam, and Adam, abdicating his responsibility to take care of her, responded to the wicked suggestion. So death entered into the world.

The God who decreed that two and two should equal four in the universe He made, and that electrons should behave in a certain way, had decreed that this man and this woman should be free to choose. He did not withhold from them the information they would need in order to choose wisely, but they did not trust Him. It was life or death that He offered. They knew better than God.

We've come now to another of the equalities. As Adam and Eve were equally responsible to God—we noted this in Genesis 1—they were equally disobedient and equally guilty, according to the story in Genesis 3.

They could never undo the damage done by their disobedience. The world was fractured. Suffering, sin, and death originated with that single defiant deed. No scurrying to retrace their steps, no amount of apologizing would smooth it over or take it away. Christians know that only the Lamb of God, slain before the foundation of the world, could accomplish that.

Eve was declaring her rights. What she saw as her rights had nothing to do with the will of God and therefore nothing to do, finally, with her happiness, sure as she was that they had.

A few months ago, when Pope John Paul visited the United States, he was confronted by angry women who accused him of depriving women of their rights by not allowing them to be ordained to the priesthood. His serenity was not disturbed by their fury. "The ordination of women," he told them, "is not a question of human rights. It is a question of the will of God." I wanted to stand up and cheer. When the pope takes his stand on scriptural principle, I take my stand with the pope.

A woman wrote to *Time*'s editor:

The Pope's reaffirmation of the ban against the ordination of women was, of course, a sexist slap in the face to all women. It was also, however, an offense to God because it

70

attributes to him a prejudice which by definition he cannot have. God gave women equal minds and hearts and an equal capacity to love and serve him. Why, then, continue to make the priesthood dependent on an anatomical difference irrelevant to the matter? Tradition is not a good enough answer.

Poor lady. Hers, not the pope's, is the slap in the face— God's face. Her notion of equality altogether rules out any appreciation of differences in gifts. Such differences, in her book, would indicate "prejudice which by definition he cannot have."

Sitting next to me during a lecture by an Evangelical who is also a feminist was my friend Joe Bayly. He and I writhed as she spoke of the equality of men and women and attempted to show that they are quite interchangeable. She seemed to feel that women had been "cheated" by the age-old prejudice that condemned them to the care of husband, home, and children. Joe, a man with a wry sense of the absurd, leaned over to me and whispered, "I'd like to have a baby." He'll never do that. Is it prejudice that makes it impossible? Has he been cheated? If so, by whom? By society? The simple truth is that he's been given—not by society, but by a wise and loving Creator—a different set of gifts, which entails a different set of responsibilities and joys.

It was not from pure prejudice that God equipped spiders to skitter, lions to spring, and donkeys to plod. It was His concern for a universe that could function together in harmony. The part each was to play in the harmony was determined as carefully as (infinitely more carefully than) the orchestration of a symphony. God did it with generosity; He did it with love; He did it with grace. His gifts to men and women are not, any more than His gifts

71

to lions or spiders, "equal." They are complementary. They contribute to the harmony or the design. It was grace, the Bible says, which gave those differing gifts. Furthermore, the anatomical difference is very far from irrelevant to the overall plan. It is wholly and wonderfully relevant.

18

Two Theaters

Men, by acting like men, and women, by acting like women, perform a drama. Drama is one of the most powerful instruments of communication, as Hamlet recognized when, bent on proving the guilt of his father's murderer, he struck on the idea of having a play performed. As a scene similar to the murder was enacted, he would observe the suspect, who was a king:

> . . . the play's the thing,
> Wherein I'll catch the conscience of the king.

If our conscience is once "caught" by the drama of our sexuality, perhaps we'll understand more clearly than in any other way just what is at stake and how very vital it is.

In the Middle Ages actors used to travel around on wagons and stop in town squares and put on mystery plays.

They were meant to help illiterate people understand things they couldn't read about—usually religious things, since that was what mattered most.

When my husband Jim and I were working with illiterate people in the boondocks of Ecuador, we sometimes resorted to our own kind of plays—pantomimes of truth we wanted to get across. We started with spiritual truth, since it's spiritual truth that matters above all. Jim made a cross by laying two boards on the ground and then lying down on top of them, to show the Indians what crucifixion meant. Very simple, but very clear. You don't need to know very many Quichua words in order to communicate that way.

God often uses visual aids. Besides the whole panorama of the world which shows us through our five senses what He is like, He gave special demonstrations for His people, for example at Mount Sinai, when He was about to give Moses the tables of the law. He sent visual aids—cloud and lightnings, fire and smoke—and audible ones—thunder and a very loud trumpet blast. That gave the Israelites an idea of Him and His holiness that they could not have had through any amount of verbal exposition or even through the ordinary phenomena of nature.

It is in these visible and audible things that the invisible, the inaudible, and even the inexpressible, are seen and heard and expressed. They are mysterious; that is, they are unexplained.

Christianity is full of mystery. All the great doctrines of the faith are, in the last analysis, mysteries. Who can explain creation? ("He spoke and it was done.") the origin of evil? ("By one man sin entered into the world and death by sin.") the nature of God? ("God is spirit, infinite, eternal, unchangeable. . . .") the nature of man? ("made in the image of God . . . and God breathed into his nostrils the breath of life.") incarnation? ("And the Word was made flesh and dwelt among us.") passion? ("This Jesus, delivered up according to the definite plan and foreknowledge of God, you crucified and killed by the hands of lawless men.") resurrection? ("He is the beginning, the firstborn from the dead, that in everything he might be preeminent.") ascension? ("A cloud took him out of their sight.") Theology labels and describes these things. It does not explain them.

Sexuality is a mystery. It represents one of the deepest of spiritual mysteries: the relationship between Christ and the Church. We will get hold of this better if it is enacted. There are two "theaters" in which this mystery is played out: the Christian home, and the local church. This is the reason, I believe, why such clear and unequivocal instructions are issued regarding how men and women are to conduct themselves in those two places. They are actors in a play in which tremendous heavenly mysteries are being enacted on stage. We have got to stick to the parts assigned and follow the director, and in so doing we will discover, as we could not in any other way, our true nature and our destiny.

19

The Cast

The casting of the characters in this play was done by God Himself. Men, He decided, were to hold the position of authority. Women were to be subordinate. Men actually (hold on to your hat, now) represent Christ—play His part in the two earthly theaters as they relate to women. The man "is the image" or "represents the very person" of God.

An outspoken Christian woman held a workshop a few years ago on what she called egalitarian marriage. I listened with growing amazement as she described her own very workable, very satisfying fifty-fifty arrangement. Apparently with blithe disregard for the divine (she would call it merely traditional) "cast," she and her husband had sat down and, according to their individual preferences, shuffled the roles around till they felt comfortable with them. Both are sociologists. Both do housework. Everything is split two ways, and they are comfortable with that. If no paradigm had been given in Scripture, if we had been left to our own devices to work out husband-wife dynamics, it might not have looked like a bad arrangement for a while. It seemed to work for them, and they liked it that way.

But you can't do that. The parts have already been assigned. And what made my jaw drop was that the lady defended this "viable option" from Ephesians 5. I did my best to keep up with the fancy footwork she did there, but it came down to this: Paul is saying everybody submits to everybody else, period. You submit to me, I to you. "After you, my sweet Alphonse." "No, after you, Gaston." The verses which followed in my Bible—the specific ways in which godly submission is supposed to work in particular relationships—were not really important at all. Wives submitting to husbands, children to parents, slaves to masters—we can dispense with all that sort of thing. Just share. She scampered around the matter of parents submitting to children, or masters to slaves. That might have been awkward to deal with.

She allowed time for questions, and you can be sure I had one. Do you see a difference, I wanted to know, between the way a husband submits to his wife and a wife submits to her husband? Her answer was no. The positions are interchangeable, then? Yes. May I then reverse the nouns in the passage? Of course. I began to read: "Husbands, be subject to your wives as to the Lord. For the wife is the head of the husband just as the Church is the head of Christ. . . ."

She stopped me. You can't carry the analogy that far, she said.

The analogy was God's. He took the central and most intimate human relationship and showed how, if it was conducted along certain lines—that is, *in order*—it would illustrate a far deeper spiritual relationship. An analogy

77

always implies that there may be other resemblances as well.

If the husband plays the part of Christ in this drama, the wife plays the part of the Church. We're back to the business of initiation and response. Christ, the Bridegroom, initiates. The Church, the Bride, responds.

You can see why it's perilous in the extreme to take things into your own hands, rearrange or innovate or reverse the roles. It's a mystery play. You have to be very careful with mysteries. You can't always be comfortable.

What is true in the theater of the home is true also in the other theater, the local church. Christ is the true Head. Men represent His authority in the local body of believers. Women, in subjection to Christ, are subject to the *representative* authority—not because they're not competent or worthy, but quite simply because they are enacting a drama. This order *stands for* something.

20

Not Merit, but Order

Nothing that God does is unstructured.

In order to make a holy people out of the Israelites, He gave them ten major commandments and hundreds of lesser ones. "If He had wanted them to live in a world without moral absolutes," said Daniel Weiss, president of Eastern College, "He would have given them the Ten Suggestions."

He gave commandments, and He also gave them a leader. Somebody had to carry the responsibility before Him. Moses, the man He chose, was not very happy about that and offered his own suggestions:

1. The people won't believe me.
2. I'm no speaker.
3. How about sending somebody else?

God allowed his brother, Aaron, to be a "mouth" for Moses, but Moses was to be to him "as God." That's what leadership is all about.

Well, there came a day when a man named Korah led a rebellion against Moses. It was the first recorded public demonstration for "equality." It followed an incident in which a man was caught collecting firewood on the Sabbath. He was brought to Moses and Aaron, who put him in custody, not being quite sure what the penalty should be. The Lord gave the word: Stone him to death.

Korah got together 250 leaders, "well-known men," who were fed up with Moses' telling them what to do. Who did they think they were? "All the congregation are holy, every one of them, and the Lord is among them; why then do you exalt yourselves above the assembly of the Lord?"

Moses' immediate response is the mark of a real man. He fell on his face. Not in fear, certainly not in shame, but in humility. This was not a time for argument or self-vindication. "In the morning the Lord will show who is his, and who is holy . . . ," Moses said. He saw clearly that the rebellion was not a personal matter. It was rebellion against God and must be dealt with by God.

Moses, as God's man, did things in order:

Take censers, Korah and all his company; put fire in them and put incense on them before the Lord tomorrow, and the man whom the Lord chooses shall be the holy one. You have gone too far, sons of Levi! . . . is it too small a thing for you that the God of Israel has separated you from the congregation of Israel, to bring you near to himself, to do service in the tabernacle of the Lord, and to stand before the congregation to minister to them; and that he has brought you near him, and all your brethren the sons of Levi with you? And would you seek the priesthood also?

They did not like the part they were given to play. They coveted another's. As usual, a protest for "equality" sprang not from a pure love of justice, but from a fundamental hatred of superiority. For this ". . . the ground under them split asunder; and the earth opened its mouth and swallowed them up, with their households, and all the men that belonged to Korah and all their goods. . . . and the earth closed over them, and they perished from the midst of the assembly."

It was a dramatic proof that the authority of Moses and Aaron was God's authority. It carried His seal and was defended by His justice. They had not gained it by merit. They were given it for the sake of order.

The parallels with what is happening today are striking. Women protest that rule and submission are curses which deprive them of "personhood," that they themselves are thereby made second-class citizens. "Who do you think you are?" they say to men who defend what is (often scornfully) called a traditional view. "Biblical" feminists label as "carnal" the hierarchical view of male-female relationships where authority resides with the men.

It sounds reasonable at first to say, "All the congregation are holy, every one of them, and the Lord is among them. . . ." This was true when Korah said it; it is true for us Christians today. We are a holy priesthood, a royal nation; we are even kings. What right have any individuals or any class of individuals to set themselves up as superior? ". . . Why then do you exalt yourselves above the assembly of the Lord?" What Korah and his mob said to Moses, women today are saying to men.

Don't be cowed by them, Pete. With all my heart I say, Don't be cowed. Stand up to them. Stand true to your calling to be a man. Real women will always be relieved and grateful when men are willing to be men.

Ask of these women the kind of questions Moses asked Korah: You have gone too far. Is it too small a thing for you that the God of Israel has separated you from men, to bring you near to Himself, to do service that no man can do, to stand before your husbands and your pastors to minister [*minister* means "serve"] to them? And would you seek equality? Would you seek the tasks I have given to men, also?

Remind them that although divine nature was His from the first, yet Jesus ". . . did not think to snatch at equality with God." He was subject. Can any woman think that she has as much right to equality with men as Jesus had with His Father?

Don't be afraid; don't be ashamed. Moses was neither. He was simply humble. He knew—and you men must remember—that it was not a matter of "setting himself up." "In the morning the Lord will show who is his, and who is holy. . . ." There's a lesson there for all twentieth-century men. It's God's authority that is being questioned. It's God's business to deal with those who rebel. "Rebellion is as the sin of witchcraft," God says. He looks for men who will see it for what it is and, in the face of social ostracism or scorn, will stand strong with Him.

21

A Take-Charge Man Is a Servant

The idea of authority is abhorrent in a lawless age. It's abhorrent to you and me, simply because we're sinners. Nobody wants anybody telling him what to do—if he thinks he already knows.

There are times, however, when even the worst of us longs for authority, because we don't know what to do. We're lost, and we want somebody to show us the way. We need leadership.

Where are the take-charge men? Cowering in corners somewhere, because of the libbers?

The idea of authority in the Bible has nothing to do with being bossy or domineering or pompous or conceited or tyrannical. In fact, it has a great deal to do with servant-hood. It requires a deep and genuine humility.

Deborah and Barak sang praise to God for the commanders of Israel ". . . who offered themselves willingly among the people. . . ." The offering up of oneself for the sake of others—this is the price of real authority. It was because Christ "humbled himself"—to the point of dying—that He is now lifted up above all others in heaven or earth. His exaltation required his humiliation. The way up is down.

You may remember a story your uncle Add used to tell. When he was dean of a small college in Pennsylvania, he learned that the walls of a certain men's dormitory were smeared with shaving cream, peanut butter, and jelly. He went over to investigate. Of course not a soul around had any idea how it could possibly have happened. In room after room he met with surprised innocence.

He had several options. He could make every man in the dormitory go to work and clean it up. He could call the custodian. It happened that the custodian was a very good worker, an amiable and therefore a very valuable man. To scrub up the mess would have been beyond the call of duty, but he would have done it. There was a third option. Add went and got a bucket and a brush and set to work himself. One by one doors opened, heads popped out, word spread of what the dean of the college was doing, and soon he was not alone in the scrub job. The power of servanthood. It commands respect. It does not *demand* it.

Jesus also "took a towel."

The kind of love described by the Greek word *agape* is defined by Edward Nason West as "a profound concern for the welfare of another without any desire to control that other, to be thanked by that other, or to enjoy the process." It gives itself. It lays down its life.

It takes a strong man or woman to lay down a life. Paul said of his co-workers Priscilla and Aquilla that they "laid down their necks," as though beneath the sword of the executioner, for his sake. That kind of strength does not fit the popular picture of a take-charge man, but it fits God's picture very well.

"When you have done all," Jesus said, ". . . you are unprofitable servants." Maybe that would be a good motto for a man to stick on the visor in his car, or for a woman to post over the sink or the typewriter.

22

The Word Spoken

Sometimes people talk about how they are "struggling with" certain things, or "working through" them, when what they really mean is that they are delaying obedience. "I have a problem with this," they say, or, "I don't feel comfortable with that yet," meaning, "Who, me? Disobedient?"

Too many Christian husbands are relegating their headship to this pigeonhole. When they've worked through all the angles, they might start doing something about it.

The authority of a man in his own home is not something progressively gained, nor is it an acquired taste. It is a summons, and no man can be "convinced" about it until he answers it. Certainty comes through willed obedience. "If any many will do his will," Jesus said, "he shall know of the doctrine, whether it be of God. . . ."

The great leaders of the Bible knew themselves called. "Now the Lord said to Abram, 'Go from your country and your kindred and your father's house.' . . . So Abram went. . . ."

To a young man who was the son of a priest in a place called Anathoth "the word of the Lord came"; "Before I formed you in the womb I knew you, and before you were born I consecrated you; I appointed you a prophet to the nations."

"Ah, Lord God!" said Jeremiah, "Behold, I do not know how to speak, for I am only a youth."

"Do not say, 'I am only a youth,'" the Lord answered, "for to all to whom I send you you shall go, and whatever I command you you shall speak. Be not afraid of them, for I am with you to deliver you. . . ."

An exiled priest named Ezekiel saw visions of God; the word of the Lord came to him, by the river Chebar, ". . . and the hand of the Lord was upon him there."

Paul opens his letter to the Romans with these words: "This letter comes to you from Paul, a servant of Christ Jesus, called as a messenger and appointed for the service of that gospel of God. . . ." In nearly every one of his letters he affirms his call—something that came to him from outside his own opinion or inclination; something "imposed" on him, which he could not dodge. It was not cause for boasting, but for submission.

It was the conviction of divine and inescapable authority that enabled Abraham and Jeremiah and Ezekiel and Paul to do the things they did for God. It was this call that made them great; it was not their personal accomplishment. They were human enough to see this and meek enough to accept it.

The commands of Scripture are clear enough: do this, don't do that. Here's a short sample list: "Stand firm." "Model your conduct." "Deny yourself." "Lay down your life." "Be strong." "Rejoice." "Behave like men."

A careful look at those shows that a man's *will* has to come into play. Sometimes we treat the royal summons as though it were an invitation that it would be more polite (or more self-effacing) to decline. We don't have that option. Men don't have the option of taking charge or not taking charge in the home and in the church. Responsibility is laid upon them. Responsibility has been the mark of a man from the moment when God shaped a woman to fit Adam's need and presented her to him and Adam recognized her and accepted her and named her. Responsibility is the refusal to drift or delay or pass the buck.

When Adam and Eve sinned, they knew at once that they were guilty. They tried to cover their nakedness with leaves and to hide themselves from the Lord God when He came walking in the garden in the cool of the day. God called the *man*. That's important. Both had taken the fruit, and it was the woman who had taken it first. But notice this: God called the man to account. "Adam, where are you?" Adam tried to evade the issue. He mentioned his nakedness, which was God's fault, after all, not his. But when God put His finger on the real issue—the forbidden fruit—Adam passed the buck. "The woman whom thou gavest to be with me, she gave me of the tree. . . ."

Adam denied his manhood. He would not accept blame either for himself or for his wife, and, when God pronounced the curse on him, it was for two reasons: "Because you have listened to the voice of your wife, and have eaten of the tree. . . ."

It is at best a misguided chivalry and at worst irresponsibility that prefers to take a backseat and let women run things. If you follow this course of action, at least you won't be called a male chauvinist, but it is disobedience.

A question often asked is, "Why is it the women who so often take the lead in spiritual things—both in church and at home? Why do the men sit back and refuse to open their mouths?" I was glad to hear one pastor say unhesitatingly, "I can answer that in one word: disobedience."

Obedience will very likely earn you nasty labels nowadays. There's nothing new about that. Obedience has never been the route to popularity. The question is simply, Who is your master? Once that's settled, you ask whether any word has been spoken. If it has, you have your orders.

23

Right and Wrong

"I believe that the most important intellectual enterprise is the distinction between right and wrong," William F. Buckley said in an interview. We must be living in a time of intellectual indolence, for the distinctions are being progressively blurred. It is popular to defend the criminal, to lay all guilt on society, to flagellate America and sympathize with any country that opposes us. What matters is not whether a thing is right, but only how it makes us feel. Since feelings are notoriously undependable, we float—like the miserable men in the space capsule—without a local vertical.

God has not left us at the mercy of feelings. He has given us directions. Specifically, those given to men are:

A man is the "head" of the woman.
He represents the very person and glory of God.
The husband is the "head" of the wife in the same way that Christ is the head of the Church and the saviour of the Body.

The husband must give his wife the same sort of love that Christ gave to the Church, when he sacrificed himself for her.

Men ought to give their wives the love they naturally have for their own bodies.

A man shall leave his father and mother and shall cleave to his wife.

Let every one of you who is a husband love his wife as he loves himself. . . .

You husbands should try to understand the wives you live with, honoring them as physically weaker yet equally heirs with you of the grace of life.

Compare the list of commands to husband with the list for wives:

The wife has no longer full rights over her own person, but shares them with her husband.

The woman reflects the person and glory of the man.

You wives must learn to adapt yourselves to your husbands, as you submit yourselves to the Lord.

The willing subjection of the Church to Christ should be reproduced in the submission of wives to their husbands. . . .

Let the wife reverence her husband.

Their role is to be receptive.

Holy women of ancient times trusted in God and were submissive to their husbands.

There you have it: the contrast between what is expected of men and what is expected of women. The lists are *different*. What is right for men is wrong for women. The roles are complementary, planned to enable husbands and wives to function together without bumping into each other or stepping on each other's toes, and in such a way as to contribute, rather than deprive, to free, rather than to shackle.

24

Authority Is a
Source of Power

I remember, when my brother Dave was very small, how he hated the ocean. My mother tried again and again to persuade him to come in and ride the waves with her, but he screamed and ran away. At the end of our stay at Belmar, New Jersey, he timidly ventured into the water. Soon he was jumping and diving, plunging and splashing through the waves in an ecstasy of delight. Suddenly it came over him that this ecstasy was about to end, for the summer was over and tomorrow we would head back to the city. He burst into tears and howled at my mother, "Why didn't you *make* me go in?"

The sooner we subject ourselves to the Lord of Life and to those He puts over us, the sooner we will find our freedom and joy. His purpose for all of us is nothing but joy in the end, for He is Love. It is worth noting that the Bible does not say God is justice, or God is power. It says He is Love. How is it possible that He would purpose anything less than our highest joy?

My mother wanted for Dave the thrill of tumbling in ocean waves. What boy would not love it, once he had tried it? But Dave refused to give himself up to her will or to the waves. They would destroy him, surely. He did not trust his mother, though he had every reason to trust her. So we deprive ourselves of infinitely more than a summer's fun, convinced that God is out to destroy us. We persist in imagining that we can will something better than the will of the Creator.

"I have come down from heaven," Jesus said, "not to do what I want, but to do the will of him who sent me. . . . My teaching is not really mine but comes from the One who sent me. . . . the man who is considering the glory of God who sent him is a true man. There can be no dishonesty about him."

"This is the pattern which man was made to imitate," C. S. Lewis writes, in *The Problem of Pain*, "and wherever the will conferred by the Creator is thus perfectly offered back in delighted and delighting obedience by the creature, there, most undoubtedly, is heaven, and there the Holy Ghost proceeds."

We had dinner last night in an elegant club atop a tower in Dallas, with a hard-driving, fast-talking, clear-thinking Christian man. He described a retreat that he organized for twenty-five friends, for the sole purpose of serious conversation. They were told at the beginning that there would be no small talk and that the group would never meet again, so it was not necessary to establish any pecking order or play any politics. Were the men all Christians? we asked. Yes, he

said, they had to be. For where there is no common authority, there can be no fruitful exchange. It was interesting to
note how, as each new topic came up, the man who was an
authority in that field was soon recognized. The Word of
God was their reference point, and the special knowledge
of each man was considered in that context; so it was the
authority of the Word, to which all were subject, that gave
unity to the group and coherence to the discussions.

The commands to men and women are our reference
points. The special gifts given to men and women find
their fullest expression within the context of God's plan.
A woman is most fully and freely a woman in relation to
a man who is willing and glad to exercise his gift of initiation. The man is most fully and freely a man in relation to
a woman who accepts her role of response.

A lugubrious illustration comes to mind. I watched on
television a herd of hippos wallowing in some great, gray,
green, greasy river in East Africa. Slowly the two spheres
of their eyelids surfaced, followed by the nostrils and mon-
strous, blunt snout. The vast bodies then billowed cumber-
somely out of the water, only to sink again. You look at a
creature like that, and you say, "There can't *be* any such
animal! It's preposterous!" And then along came a beautiful
white egret, alighted delicately on the muddy head, and
daintily picked off the bugs that tormented the hippo. What
a friendly arrangement! The hippo provided the feeding
ground; the bird provided the pest-extermination service.
Each does what the other cannot do, and they complement
each other.

So what am I doing? Comparing a man's relation to a
woman with a hippopotamus's to an egret? Well, in a manner of speaking, yes. (You thought I was about to say a
vehement no, didn't you?) Every benevolent interaction

between God's creatures, from the mating of the lowliest crustacean to the encounters between men and angels, speaks to me. It speaks of a God who is the Giver of Life, who thought of all the possible ways in which His creatures should live and function in harmony.

"It is the passion for life and its largeness that is at the root of rebellion," wrote P. T. Forsyth. "Subordination is divine. The principle has its roots in the cohesion of the eternal Trinity itself. To recognize no lord or master, this is satanic. I insist on the Christian principle, drawn from the very nature of God and essential to the masculinity and femininity which he has made. Without the spirit of subordination there is no true piety, no manly nobility and no womanly charm."

In deadly opposition to this Christian principle stands the verdict of feminism, "Rule and submission are curses." No wonder Germaine Greer said, "If there is a God, I'd be in guerrilla warfare with Him."

25

Initiation into Manhood

Some of the difficulties in our society are due, I think, to the lack of any ceremony to mark the distinction between adolescence and manhood. Primitive societies commonly require some form of initiation. The Nuer people of the southern Sudan make tribal markings on the foreheads of young men by cutting deep lines, so that scars remain. Outside the women's domain, the boy is made to lie on the ground with his head in steer dung while the cuts are made. The blood pours out, and he is not to flinch or even so much as to grimace. A bull is castrated at the same time, and the boy takes the bull's name, dances with him, and thus identifies with the animal that has forfeited its sexuality for him. Never again is the boy permitted to sleep in his mother's hut or to milk a cow. He is now a man, qualified to fight, hunt, and marry.

Many ancient myths and legends tell of a hero who must go through a dark passage or ordeal of some kind, struggling with the wild beasts or dragons, overcoming evil and emerging victorious—into new life, new knowledge, new responsibility. There is a sense in which every major crisis in the human cycle—birth, puberty, marriage, and death—represents this passage. The old must be renounced (the warmth and security of the womb, for example), the suffering of the transition endured (the birth itself—painful and frightening), all opposition overcome (learning to cope with light, noise, and cold, learning to breathe), and new life entered into. In puberty the man leaves behind the innocence of childhood; he must prove his ability to endure and overcome; and he enters into new life, new knowledge and the new responsibility of being a man. It is entirely possible that one of the reasons men are not men in modern society is that they have no puberty rites. The closest they come to such a thing is in sports, and the trouble with sports is that they only imitate life in a highly controlled and artificial way. Men need to prove themselves somehow, and since there are no animals to kill for food, enemies to scalp or spear, or physical hardship to be endured in order to survive in civilized life, they have chosen to resort to contrived conditions: games, scuba diving, hang gliding, rock climbing, surfing, and even gambling. Risk is a necessary ingredient for the proof of manhood, but the built-in weakness of sports is that the risks are unnecessary. Except in the case of professional athletes, sports have nothing to do with providing food and shelter for a family.

It is not as though life itself cannot provide the tests. Suffering awaits us all, in some form or another, and though by various means we may postpone and evade it for a while, sooner or later we must come to terms with it. "If [young men] would but await what will come, and accept the thing that is sent them, it would make men of them in half the time," wrote George MacDonald. "There is more to be had out of the ordained oppositions in things than from the smoothest going of the world's wheels."

You've experienced a few of the minor "ordained oppositions"—the troubles referred to in the introduction to this book: girl friends, cars, exams. What are they for, if not to make a man of you, Pete?

The real test of manhood, it seems to me, is not the Boston Marathon, but "the race that is set before *you*," mentioned in Hebrews 12. Paul wrote to the young man Timothy, "Take time and trouble to keep yourself spiritually fit. Bodily fitness has a certain value, but spiritual fitness is essential, both for this present life and for the life to come."

It is not to our peers that we need to prove our maturity. "I solemnly charge you in the sight of God and Christ Jesus and the holy angels to follow these orders with the strictest impartiality. . . ." While you may not be charged with precisely the same duties as Timothy, it is to the same tribunal that you will have to answer. It is an awesome tribunal: God, Christ Jesus, and the holy angels.

26

The Route to Life

The Bible is full of models of God's idea of manhood. Abraham took the huge risk of believing God and obeying His shocking command, "Go from your country and your kindred and your father's house to the land that I will show you." It was an initiation ceremony. If he wanted to be a man under God, he had to submit to the ordeal. He submitted and went.

Talk about forsaking the comfortable and familiar and going through perils! Can you picture his entourage, probably at least sixty people, "and all their possessions which they had gathered, and the persons that they had gotten in Haran . . ."?

When you see wilderness such as that country from Haran to Canaan, and the Negeb, you are aware that the risk Abraham took was very real and frightening. What if they starved? What if there wasn't water for the people and animals? What if there were hostile people? They did, in fact, experience famine. There was a feud between Abraham's and Lot's herdsmen. Lot was captured. Abraham experienced "a dread and great darkness" at one point. There was a tribal marking. God established the covenant of circumcision, a specifically male sign, to bind Abraham and his descendants to God forever. The analogies go on and on; not once, but again and again he went through "passages." The greatest ordeal of his life surely was when he was asked to offer up his only son as a sacrifice on an altar. He did not shrink even from that, but passed the tests with flying colors. A real man.

The mark of the man Daniel was self-discipline. He resisted the king's rich menu; he kept regular times of prayer. He reached the position of being "distinguished above all the other presidents and satraps, because an excellent spirit was in him . . . ," which caused jealousy among his rivals, who then reported to the king his devotion to his God. This resulted in his being thrown into a den of lions, from which he emerged "and no kind of hurt was found upon him, because he had trusted in his God."

David was another one who went through the tests of manhood. "All Israel and Judah loved him because he took the field at their head."

It was their willingness to give up themselves for the sake of God and other people that proved them real men. Sports make a poor substitute for such rites. They are not for the sake of God and others, but for the sake of oneself, for glory and for gain.

The life of Jesus interprets for us in every way the whole meaning of life and death, for His life on earth was bound up always with death.

"Let Christ Jesus Himself be your example as to what your attitude should be. For He, Who had always been God by nature, did not cling to His prerogatives as God's Equal, but stripped Himself of all privilege by consenting to be a slave by nature and being born as a mortal man." Here is the supreme paradigm—the deliberate act of the will of Jesus, "annihilating" or "dispossessing" Himself, which is what the root word means. He stripped Himself. Often tribal rites require a man to be stripped—a symbol of the casting off of all that is connected with the old life. Jesus came, as Henry Barraclough's hymn puts it:

> Out of the ivory palaces
> Into a world of woe,
> Only His great eternal love. . . .
> Made my Savior go.

The humiliation of the Lord of the universe restricting Himself to the womb of a peasant girl in the village of Nazareth, then His coming into the world, into a stable, as a helpless, squalling infant is described in these words of Richard Crashaw:

> That the Great Angel-blinding light should shrink
> His blaze, to shine in a poor shepherd's eye;
> That the unmeasur'd God so low should sinke,
> As Pris'ner in a few poor rags to lye,
> That from his Mother's Breast he milke should
> drinke,
> Who feeds with Nectar Heaven's faire family,
> That a vile Manger his low Bed should prove,
> Who in a Throne of stars Thunders above;
> That he whom the Sun serves, should faintly peepe
> Through clouds of Infant Flesh! That He, the old
> Eternall Word should be a Child, and weepe;

101

That He who made the fire, should feare the cold,
That Heaven's high Majesty His Court should
keepe
In a clay cottage, by each blast control'd;
That Glories self should serve our Griefs and feares,
And free Eternity submit to years,
Let our overwhelming wonder be.

Even His birth was tied up with dying. Every minute of His earthly life was a death for Him, every minute His offering up of Himself and His will, yet, as He told His disciples, doing the will of the Father was *food* to Him.

We see in His earthly life a whole new way of being with people, of loving and serving them at the expense of Himself. It was *out of* this daily dying, *because of* it and its culmination in physical death as a common criminal, that Life came. He is the Resurrection. He is Life. He wants to give us Life.

That's what it takes to be fully a man, Pete. You must share the life of Christ. Without Him you can do nothing—simple as that: absolutely nothing. But, with Him—everything. A man's willingness to offer up his life, for his wife or for anybody else who happens to need him, is not the end of everything. It's only the end of himself.

I know it's true. There are times when everything in us resists taking the step forward that must be taken. Think of Abraham's actual packing up and saying good-bye and starting out on that wilderness journey. Think of the decision that Daniel made after he heard the king's decree. Was he going to go right ahead and open his windows toward Jerusalem and kneel down where he could so easily be spotted and take the risk that was a matter of life or death? Everything in these men must have said, *No!* Every thing except one: their desire to please God. Don't forget that

102

Daniel was a young man—very likely your age—with the same sort of ambitions and hungers and temptations.

I have talked to someone in the past few days who is being asked to say no to himself in a most radical and traumatic way. His pride, his reputation, and his self-image are on the line. He wants, almost viciously, to say yes, but he knows it has to be no. What I wish with all my heart I could make him see is that the world will not, in fact, fall to pieces when he says it. In fact, it won't be the end of anything except himself, and the end of himself will be freedom and joy and light and gaiety—yes, I'm sure of it—gaiety! But that gaiety will come, not in spite of, but actually because of, that relinquishment. The no is the pre-requisite. "The men who are signed by the cross," wrote G. K. Chesterton, "go gaily in the dark."

Life comes, not in spite of, but because of death. God was able to accomplish His will through Abraham, not in spite of Abraham's sufferings, and sacrifices, but because of them. Daniel shines as a model of faith (and gives life to our faith), not in spite of the ordeal of the lions' den that he braved, but because of it. It took that kind of death to show a living faith.

He who is fully a man has relinquished his right to himself. "Have my blood," Jim Elliot wrote in his college journal. "Have it all. Let it be poured out for the life of the world." When the chance came to take a big risk in obedience to God, he took it at once—he went "gaily"! I doubt that he remembered the words of that prayer, but the matter had been settled long before. The route to Life had to be the Way of Death.

27

Authority Is Fitting

We can rest assured that whatever gifts are appropriate to the job God wants us to do will be given to us.

Men have different gifts, but it is the same Spirit who gives them. There are different ways of serving God, but it is the same Lord who is served. God works through different men in different ways, but it is the same God who achieves his purposes through them all. The Spirit openly makes his gift to each man, so that he may use it for the common good. . . . you are together the body of Christ. . . .

A body needs a head. It needs a source of authority. Christ is the source of all authority.

In fact, every single thing was created through, and for, Him. He is both the First Principle and the Upholding Principle of the whole scheme of creation. And now He is the Head of the body which is composed of all Christian people. Life from nothing began through Him, and life from the dead began through Him, and He is, therefore, justly called the Lord of all.

Now here is an amazing thing. The husband, we are told in Ephesians, is the head of the wife, "*in the same way* that Christ is the head of the Church and savior of the Body."

Countless pages have been written to prove that the "headship" of the husband carries no connotation whatsoever of authority. The husband is merely the "source." It's quite true that he is the woman's source—that is, her source of being—if she was made out of one of his very bones, but the analogy being used in this passage is that of the relationship of a person's head to his body. It's the source, not of being, but of power and of authority. The arms and legs take orders from the head. You can cut off an arm or a leg, and the body can still function. But, cut off a head, and the body is finished.

If a man is "head" of his wife *in the same way* that Christ is Head of the Church, he must bear authority over her. To deny this is to empty the analogy of its central meaning.

Christ's willingness to be Head over the Church was a part of His submission to the Father. A man's willingness to be the head of his wife is a matter of *submission*—to Christ. For her to oppose his authority is to oppose God. For him to refuse it is to disobey God.

Each receives the gifts which fit him or her for the job. What we are—men or women—determines what we do. The secular view of sexuality sees it as a material object to be used in any way we choose. The Christian sees his or her sex first as a gift, potent and undeniable, originating in the thought and love of God. It is what he or she is and profoundly determines what he or she does, for the gift fits him or her for the job—not merely the job of propagating the species, but of being a man or a woman in the world, in the church, and at home.

It is worth noting that recent studies in ethnology, anthropology, endocrinology and experimental psychology are converging to support what mothers and poets have known all along—that men and women are not only built differently, but think and act differently. Two Stanford psychologists, Karl Pribram and Dianne McGuinness, have concluded that women are "communicative" animals, being more oriented toward people, and that men are "manipulative," being more interested in things. When boys and girls have been given three-dimensional objects to manipulate and take apart, boys have overwhelmingly outperformed girls.

The notion that behavioral differences in boys and girls are solely the result of environment has all but collapsed as evidence is building up of "a genetic component in certain kinds of behavior—for example, aggression or nurturance—that have traditionally been identified as masculine or feminine. . . . In no human culture ever studied has the female been found more aggressive than the male."

It is *fitting* that one should lead and the other follow. Things work better that way, and it's a relief not to have to vote on who's going to be the leader. (What a time-consuming business that would be, in our house!) God has it all worked out, and, if we fall in with His plan, things will be done as He loves them done: decently and in order.

When Paul writes to the Colossians "And whatever work you may have to do, do everything in the Name of the Lord Jesus, thanking God the Father through Him," he says immediately what sort of "work" he's talking about: Wives, adapt! Husbands, love!

Anybody who has honestly tried either for any length of time knows it's work. It's no use pretending that we're doing things "in the name of the Lord Jesus" if we're not doing them His way.

"What men do on their own initiative," writes Mircea Eliade in *The Sacred and the Profane*, "what they do without a mythical model, is profane, therefore vain, illusory, unreal." We've been given the true model. In Him the principles and paradigms must be sought and recognized.

28

Who Does the Wooing?

If it is fitting, Pete, that man carry authority not only because he is genetically composed to be the aggressor, but also because he is given spiritual responsibility; the question of "wooing" is not irrelevant.

A young woman approached a man who was deep in study in the seminary library. She knelt beside his chair and shyly slid a dime onto the table next to his books.

"It's all I have," she whispered, "but if you have a nickel, we could share a cup of coffee." The man, reluctant not only to be interrupted in his studies, but also to be placed in such an indefinable position, saw her desperation, went with her, and paid for two cups of coffee.

You could top that story twenty times over, I'm sure. I remember your telling me of the night you were working for a catering firm at a fancy wedding party. One of the more attractive young females asked you to dance. This was an awkward position, indeed, for she could not possibly have mistaken you for a guest: You were wearing your waiter's white coat and black bow tie. Being both a gentleman and conscientious, you turned her down.

Women are doing too much of the seeking nowadays. I am floored by their tactics, but perhaps nobody has ever taken the trouble to explain to them why they are inappropriate. I hear of notes placed in seminary mailboxes; phone calls; "accidental" meetings in hallways, which seem mysteriously to recur. Women students ask me how they can "relate" to the "brothers." It is hard to know where to start to answer that question. Several fallacies lie behind it. They use a term, *brothers*, which describes a spiritual relationship, to cover what they hope will turn out to be something more personal and emotional. They claim that it is fellowship they desire, but they could have that with their dorm mates. It's fellows they're interested in, bless their hearts, and I couldn't be more sympathetic! I *like* men. It's their assuming the responsibility that I deplore. They are trying to snare a "brother" into a "relationship." They would do much better to direct their energies toward trusting God and leave the wooing to the man God wants them to have.

"You mean I'm not supposed to do *anything*?" women sometimes say to me.

"That's not what I said," I tell them. "Trusting God is doing the greatest thing anybody can do. Trusting God to take care of your love life (I know from experience) is a rigorous daily exercise of faith."

It is perfectly true that Christians *are* brothers and sisters. Even a wife can be called a sister. "Have we not power," Paul asked, "to lead about a sister, wife . . . ?" Phillips translates this, "May we not travel with a Christian wife . . . ?"

109

showing that *Christian* is synonymous with *sister* or *brother*. Older women, Paul told Timothy, were to be treated not as sisters, but as mothers. He was describing relationships within the family of God. To be children of one heavenly Father makes us relatives.

This points up the second fallacy that lies behind the women's question "How can we relate?" There is a technicality here in the use of the word that is not quite so trivial as may appear. When used transitively, the word *relate* means "to show," not "to create," a relationship, as in, for example, "to relate theory and practice." Lately the word seems to have come to mean "to connect," "to associate with," or even "to approve of." (A girl who did not agree with something I said told me she "could not relate to it," meaning, I think, that she did not approve of it, disassociated herself from it, denied all connection.)

The relationship between Christian brothers and sisters is not something we create. It's already established. We are members one of another. We *are related*, so the efforts of the lonely, eager women I've described are misdirected.

I don't claim to have the Law of Sinai on my side with regard to the rules of courtship, much less of the now nearly defunct custom of dating. But surely the paradigms of Christ's relationship to His own Bride have some bearing on the way a Christian man and woman should approach marriage. If a husband is to love his wife *as* Christ loves the Church, if he is to be her head in the same way in which Christ is the Head of the Church, he is going to have to do the seeking, the wooing, the winning. Things were undoubtedly much less strained when parents or other older and wiser people made the choice of marriage partners. Arranged marriages generally worked better than the majority of modern "spontaneous" ones. But we are stuck with the present system, and the best way for a man to thread his way through its terrible difficulties is to study the paradigm. "He drew me with cords of love and thus he bound me to him" as the hymn says.

The seeking, the wooing, the winning, while not helped anymore by time-honored and wise custom—for the customs have been discarded—can be done sanely, chastely, and prayerfully. The Lord has promised wisdom to all who ask it. He has promised guidance to those who are willing to accept the way He chooses. He has promised to fulfill the desires of all who fear Him.

An anonymous hymn describes Christ's wooing:

> I sought the Lord, and afterward I knew
> He moved my soul to seek Him, seeking me;
> It was not I that found, O Saviour true,
> No, I was found of Thee.

The Bible often speaks of God's seeking the love of His people as a lover seeks the beloved. I have already noted Ezekiel's comparing Jerusalem to an unwanted baby, thrown into an open field and then rescued, later growing into beautiful womanhood. ". . . I plighted my troth to you and entered into a covenant with you, says the Lord God, and you became mine." Ephraim is compared to a child who is taught to walk, taken up in God's arms, healed, and led with "cords of compassion, with the bands of love." This imagery again points to the transcendence of the sexual relationship. Surely an effort to acknowledge that transcendence whenever possible—even on so apparently casual an occasion as a date—will not be misplaced, since dating is at least an initial approach to marriage and perhaps the only even remotely formal one in our society.

29

Authority Means Sacrifice

"What if she turns me down?" Breathes there a man so cock-sure of himself that he has never asked this question?

The initiator always takes risks. Christ took them for us. "He came into his own world, and his own people would not accept him."

One of the handsomest young men I know explained that he was dating a certain girl simply because he was lonely, and she made it obvious she was available, and he was not afraid he might be rejected. Having heard the complaints of the girls who wait in vain in the dormitories for a single telephone call, I found it hard to believe that this dazzling man feared rejection.

Yet all of us do. To aim at loving instead of at being loved requires sacrifice. Love reaches out, willing to be turned down or inconvenienced, expecting no personal reward, waiting only to give.

But that's an impossible standard for a human being's love, you'll say. You're not Everlasting Love—far from it. The unavoidable fact, however, is that this "impossible" standard *is* the standard. There isn't any other standard by which we are to measure our love. ". . . love one another as I have loved you," Jesus said, and Paul said, "The husband must give his wife the same sort of love that Christ gave to the Church, when he sacrificed himself for her. Christ gave himself to make her holy, having cleansed her [think of the discarded baby in the field] through the baptism of his Word—to make her an altogether glorious Church [think of how that baby grew into a beautiful woman] in his eyes. She is to be free from spots. . . ." The requirements go on and on.

Ponder this love, Pete. It's a far cry from the soupy, selfish sentiment the world calls love. It's got nothing to do with it, really. It's a high and holy summons to forget yourself.

"Forget myself? No way." That's a normal human response. There is no way, of course, except by the grace of God. We're called to participate with Christ in His own work, to love with His love, to do what He does to and for one another. There's no way in the world to do it alone. We do it because He lives His life in us.

When you find yourself saying, "But isn't it about time I got a little appreciation; doesn't *she* have any responsibility? Hey, I'm doing it all!" it's time to review the standard, "the same sort of love Christ gave."

You want your wife to submit? Then take a long, steady look at the sort of love Christ gave. It was based on self-sacrifice. That is the basis for authority. It starts with sacrifice. It is maintained by sacrifice. Napoleon once said that he had built an empire on force, while Jesus built one on love. For two millennia since, there has never been a time when there were not hundreds of thousands willing to die for Him. No force on earth can compare with the force of sacrificial love.

It won't do merely to "go with your feelings." There's no telling where your feelings will take you. Sometimes you'll feel like quitting or evading. Henpecked husbands are usually those who have yielded to this temptation. If the little woman wants it, whatever it is—from a dishwasher to control over the checkbook—give it to her. So, by default, these easygoing men find themselves in subjection, instead of in charge.

There is the opposite temptation: to bulldoze. Unsure of their authority, weak men assert it obnoxiously.

"What would you do," I recently asked a well-known theologian, "if your wife defied you and, for example, refused to answer when you asked where she had been?"

"I am more inclined to persuade than to demand," he said.

Neither the one extreme (defaulting) nor the other (bulldozing) marks the true man. The true man knows when he is up against something too big for him and needs help. He is driven to the only One who knows how to love like this, and asks for help, on his knees. This will free him from the rage that often follows defiance and from the sense of helplessness and hurt pride. He holds his wife up to Christ as he loves and prays for her. He makes *her* a sacrifice and an offering when he relinquishes force. He offers himself as well, holy and acceptable to God.

There would surely be far fewer divorces if men knew how to love sacrificially. Most of the rationalizations offered as reasons for divorce center around the happiness of the two people. They've changed since they got married at age twenty-one. They are no longer the man and woman they were then. They've grown apart. One or the other is not finding fulfillment. They never "really loved" each other. (Is anyone's memory to be trusted to that extent? If people hate each other, they can't possibly remember what it was like to love.) The relationship just isn't working. They would be freer apart. "To waste our lives would be a sin," as the song goes. And so on.

Divorce is not an option. God hates it. In freedom you choose a woman; and you then bind yourself, by vows before God and witnesses, that you will love, honor, and cherish her till death you do part. You promise to forsake all others.

Nobody can stick to such vows in his own strength. "The arm of flesh will fail you. Ye dare not trust your own," as the old hymn says. Those who overcome do so not by force of will or strength of superior character, but by the blood of the Lamb. *Sacrifice* was required of His love for us. Nothing less than sacrifice will be required of us if it is our serious intention to love for a lifetime.

30

Leadership through Suffering

Doctors generally agree that men are not very good at suffering. A friend of mine says that when her husband gets a cold or a little bout of winter flu, she doesn't mind it when he goes to bed. She doesn't mind carrying up the newspaper and the hot lemonade and tuning the TV for him. She doesn't mind making chicken soup for him. "But, when the groaning starts . . . !" That's what she minds.

Another friend had a mastectomy, and when I called to try to console her, telling her I sympathized with the horror she must feel at being thus mutilated, she laughed and said, "Oh, I guess I haven't even thought about that!

I'm fine, really." I mentioned what doctors say about women's ability to endure pain, and she laughed again. "I think it must be because women are so used to being miserable!"

Whether or not any of that is true, I know that leadership is developed through suffering. The men who are to be leaders must learn how. There once lived a man who relinquished a position far above all angels and became inferior to them in order to be subject to pain and death, "that he should, by God's grace, taste death for every man. . . ." He tasted it every day of His life on earth, doing not what He wanted to do, but what His Father wanted Him to do. He grew up in a common peasant home, probably worked as a carpenter for many obscure years, and in the last two or three years of His brief life was an itinerant teacher who, as George MacDonald says, "in the broad face of prejudiced respectability, truth-hating hypocrisy, commonplace religion, and dull book-learning," declared "I am the Life." Every event of His earthly life was a taste of death. One of the earliest incidents will serve to illustrate this. He went to the synagogue in Nazareth, where He had been brought up, and when handed the scroll, by the servant of the synagogue, He stood up and read from Isaiah 61. He sat down and said, "Today this Scripture has been fulfilled in your hearing." The grace ("pure heavenly gift that can be neither demanded nor forced, and loveliness, delicate, mobile beauty," Romano Guardini's definition) with which He spoke amazed the hearers. Holiness was in their midst, the presence of God Himself, yet their response was a challenge and an objection: "Isn't this Joseph's son?" How like the rest of us: Instead of confronting truth directly, we attack the one who speaks it and seek to undermine

117

his credentials in order to evade the sword that pierces to the marrow.

Jesus knew what it meant to be ignored, opposed, misunderstood and jeered at. He was at the last betrayed by a disciple, forsaken by those closest to Him, captured by a mob, insulted, lied about, imprisoned, beaten, slapped, stripped, and finally, classified as a common criminal and nailed to a wooden cross.

"It was right and proper," says the writer to the Hebrews, "that in bringing many sons to glory, God . . . should make the Leader of their salvation a Perfect Leader through the fact that He suffered."

A man who is to be a leader must prepare for leadership in the same way Jesus prepared: by being willing to suffer. The word sounds almost strange to modern ears. What do we know, in this wonderful country, of suffering? As a nation we have never known real want. We have not been persecuted. There has been no war on our own soil during our lifetime. There have been, of course, earthquakes, floods, the recent devastating eruption of Mount Saint Helens, in Washington. There is always illness. There are riots and strikes and crime. Violent death threatens us on the highways, in the cities. Even though, through television, we have a vastly increased awareness of the possibilities of disaster, healthy minded people do not lie awake nights, wondering which kind will strike them. Most of us, admittedly, have our times of anxiety, when the imagination takes over and we picture the bottom falling out in various ways. But what is it that the godly man is to *do* about this thing called suffering?

I don't believe he is to go out looking for it. He makes certain choices in life: a career, a wife, a place to live. If he is mature and responsible, he accepts the conditions of those choices, even though some of them entail suffering of one kind or another. Rarely do we think of the ordinary "breaks" of life as suffering; yet the moral, emotional, physical, and financial responsibilities that any ordinary man takes on, if he has a wife or a wife and children, are a good place to start. Job hunting, taxes, promotion, competition, and family headship—not to mention the daily realities of commuting; maintaining house, yard, and car in order; being a faithful church member; and paying the bills—make up a heavy load for a human being to carry on his shoulders. No wonder Thoreau described most men as leading lives of "quiet desperation." Anxiety over these burdens gives people cancer, heart attacks, ulcers, and a long list of other maladies. Despair leads them to divorce and suicide. A Christian knows that there is One who can make the yoke easy.

To *suffer* simply means "to bear under." A leader is a man who does not groan under burdens, but takes them as a matter of course, allows them, tolerates them—and with a dash of humor. He knows how to keep his mouth shut about his difficulties and how to live a day at a time, doing quietly what needs doing at the moment. People will follow that sort of man.

Again I have to say you don't do it alone. Perhaps I seem to be belaboring the point, but lest the "rules" for leadership appear impossibly supernatural, we need to recall constantly that it is Christ who calls us; it is Christ who enables us; it is Christ who promises His presence and His strength. Whom did He call to be disciples? Weren't they quite ordinary men? None was outstanding, so far as we know, before his call to discipleship. It was not unusual gifts or an unusual spirituality or any position of temporal success already gained that drew Jesus' attention to them.

119

He spent a night in prayer to His Father, prior to the decision, and then, in accord with the Father's will, issued the call. I pray, Pete, that you (and others who may read this) will answer the call to be willing to suffer in order to lead, to be last in order to be first.

31

Trustees of the Mystery

The husband is the head of the wife. The Book doesn't say he *ought to be* or he *must work at it and become*. It says he *is*, in the same way that Christ is the Head of the Church. No matter how many times I go over this stupendous assertion of Paul's, I don't comprehend it. Paul said it was a great mystery.

In another passage he speaks of being "trustees of the secrets of God," or "stewards of the mysteries." He's speaking primarily of ministers or apostles, I think; but if a husband is head of his wife, he's also responsible for a mystery—responsible to order his life and their lives together, according to what is being represented.

Yes, hummm. All very theological and profound, I hear you saying. But what's that got to do with living under the same roof, sitting at the same table, and sleeping in the same bed with a woman?

The answer is everything. It has everything to do with the business of marriage, with doing what Christ does.

"Laying down your life" for her as Christ laid down His life for His Bride means, to begin with, choosing to relinquish your privacy and your independence. This woman will be into everything.

"Let a woman in your life," sang Rex Harrison in *My Fair Lady*, "and your serenity is through!"

> She'll have a booming, boisterous family
> That will descend on you en masse.
> She'll have a large Wagnerian mother
> With a voice that shatters glass.

Maybe it's not always quite that bad, but your house will not be your own. It's *ours*. You have to learn to say "Come on over to *our* place, " not "*my* place." (And it will be a good idea to check with your wife *before* you issue any invitations!) You'll find things don't stay where you put them. This has its advantages if you happen to be the kind of man who needs to be picked up after. You can drop things on the floor, but the house stays neat in spite of you. It can be infuriating, however, to realize that the car keys are not on top of the washing machine, where you left them, and that the tickets to the ball game are no longer in the pocket of your golf jacket; the golf jacket has been to the cleaners.

Remind yourself, before you blow your stack, that you invited this woman into your life. One of the sacrifices love makes is privacy. Think of the eternal harassment God opened Himself to by creating us in the first place and then by inviting us to be His Bride!

Another analogy is this mystery is the name you give her. God chose the people of Israel to bear His name. The prophets refer often to God's people as being "called by His name." A woman, unless she is a feminist or has no idea that it makes any important difference, takes her husband's name. She signifies by that that she accepts him as her identity. She will always be known as so-and-so's wife; and she loses her own name, to all practical purposes. I heard a widow just last week say that when her husband died, she had "no identity." "Why not?" I wanted to ask. She was still the same woman she was before he died. She still had his name. She was now so-and-so's widow, rather than his wife, and that is her identity. She didn't really need to "do something" to demonstrate that she was somebody.

We belong to Christ. We bear His name. We're Christians. That identity can get you persecution and derision, sometimes, but it *is* who we are. You give your name, with all it means, to the woman who becomes your wife; and she is from then on identified with who you are.

A husband asks his wife to share his destiny. What is his becomes hers; where he goes she'll go; what he suffers she'll suffer; his privileges will be her privileges. She doesn't often see in advance the price she will have to pay. She sees the delights. But both are her portion. That is why marriage vows are so necessary. They remind both partners that the story will not be all "for better," "for richer," "in health." They promise to stand by each other in case of the opposites: for worse, for poorer, in sickness.

When Jesus called disciples to Himself, He reminded them that He had no place to lay His head. Were they willing to share that destiny? They had to settle that question first, but it wasn't the whole story. "If we suffer, we shall also reign with him . . ." is the glorious ending. Part of Christ's destiny is kingship. "Son, thou art ever with me, and all that I have is thine."

It's a two-way street. If a man gives up his privacy and his independence, he also has someone to come home to. She's there. She may be harried and preoccupied at times, but he can sound off to her. He knows he matters to somebody. Though he might once in a while wake suddenly in the night and wonder what ever possessed him to take on the responsibility of this woman sleeping beside him and of all debts contracted by her, as well as the responsibility of the children (and maybe the in-laws!), at other times he will feel it was not too high a price to pay.

"I know you think it's worth it," I said to Lars (for he lets me know that in many ways). "Can you give me some examples of why?"

He looked surprised. "Don't know if I've had those thoughts in the night, but if a man does wake with the thoughts you mention, all he'd need to do then would be to reach over and feel her, warm in the bed beside him, and remember what it was like when he had to sleep alone. When he drives into the driveway after a hard day's work, he can remember what it was like to come home to an empty house, where nobody was waiting, there was no supper cooking, nobody to talk to."

To *husband* means, as I have noted, "to take care of," "to cherish." As Christ cherishes His own Body, His Bride—that is, us—so as man cherishes a woman: holds her dear, values her highly, treats her tenderly. Too much to expect of man? Think of how you treat your own body. You have no difficulty holding it dear, valuing it highly, treating it tenderly. Give your wife the same kind of breaks.

Pay attention. Notice when she's tired or cold or upset or needing your arms around her.

"The love a man gives his wife is the extending of his love for himself to enfold her. Nobody ever hates or neglects his own body; he feeds it and looks after it. And that is what Christ does for His Body, the Church."

The tabernacle, in ancient times, was a mysterious representation of certain eternal concepts that Israel was not yet equipped to understand. It was Lesson One, "a holy place in this world for the eternal God," Hebrews 9 says. "Fixed representations," "full of meaning," a "picture of the present time," "ceremonies . . . only intended to be valid until the time when Christ should establish the truth."

The priests were the stewards of those mysteries. Likewise, the husband, as priest in his home, is charged with the guarding of mysteries. It's his business to remember what marriage represents—the heavenly union of Christ and His Bride—and to pay attention to the everyday means of living this out with the woman God gave him.

Often the attempt will seem so laughable, such a travesty, so ludicrously unlike what it stands or, that both will wonder how God could possibly have laid such a solemn task at their door. If the toast is burning, the phone ringing, the baby is pouring milk down the mother's back, and the husband is frantically trying to find his briefcase in time to make the car pool, he will not, at the moment, feel much like a "trustee of the mysteries." But he is one nevertheless. "Nobody chooses for himself the honor of being a high priest, but he is called by God to the work . . ." the writer to the Hebrews says. "Thus we see that the

Christ did not choose for Himself the glory of being High Priest. . . ."

You shouldn't choose it for yourself, Pete, but if you remember that you're called by God to the work and if you witness to that calling in the home you establish, it will be a saving, even a life-transfiguring, reality.

32

Courtesy

When I walked into a meeting room where ten men were seated, three stood. Etiquette required only one to have stood, if a meeting had been in progress, but it hadn't started. The three were observing a *ceremony*, a formal act established by custom as proper to an occasion. The seven who sat did not observe it, because they didn't know any better or because they knew better, but for reasons of their own, rejected the custom or because they were not paying attention or because—and this reason is a common one and reveals an important fundamental attitude—they didn't want to look silly.

I asked a seminary class how many of those who were married ever helped their wives in or out of their chairs at the table if there was no company present. There wasn't a single hand. The subject of my lecture that day was courtesy, so I "socked it to 'em" for two hours about what courtesy ought to signify in a Christian home. Is it a lot of foolish and meaningless conventions that Christians, in the interest of honesty and simplicity, can well dispense with? I don't think it is, and I tried to show them why. I gave them a week to think it over, and then I asked again for a show of hands. "Is there anybody here who, as a result of last week's lecture, has altered, in the smallest detail, his treatment of his wife?" There was not one hand. You don't need the lecture, Pete. You've always been unselfishly courteous. On second thought, though, perhaps you haven't considered the rationale behind good manners, and I hope I can do a better job of convincing you than I did that class.

Courtesy is sacrificial symbolism. We've been talking about sacrifice, which runs deep through all Christian truth. "Every High Priest is appointed to offer gifts and make sacrifices," Hebrews tells us. As Christians, as "priests" to God, we, too, make sacrifices: our bodies, first of all; and our praise, our thanksgiving and our faith. These are all called sacrifices in the New Testament. It goes without saying that we human beings haven't got a thing to offer up to God, except what we've been given; and your manhood is a gift that you offer back to Him. It's also a gift you offer your wife. Without that offering, she is not free to be fully a woman; for to be fully a woman means to respond, to receive, to be acted upon, to follow. You've got to give her the gift of your manhood—initiating, cherishing, leading. This is what women want, in their heart of hearts.

I say that courtesy is sacrificial symbolism because each act is a very small sign that you are willing to give your life for hers. When you pass the salt to her, you're saying, "You first." When you help her on with her coat, you're not saying, "You're too weak to do it yourself"; you're saying that you're willing to take trouble for her. "Good morning, darling, how are *you* this morning?" is a convention, of course. (Conventions have only become conventions because they have worked and have meant something for a long time.) But if you think about it, you could, by that conventional greeting, be meaning, "My feelings are not my primary interest this morning. Yours are." Sir Walter Raleigh's putting down his cloak in a puddle for the sake of his queen was an inconvenience, to say the least. Love is willing to be inconvenienced.

It is a mistake to dismiss customs by saying, "It's only cultural." It *is* cultural, but it is within the context of our culture that we communicate selfishness or unselfishness. Do you remember the story of Jesus having dinner at the house of a Pharisee named Simon? When a "woman of the city who was a sinner" offered a gesture of adoration—washing Jesus' feet with tears, drying them with her hair, and then pouring perfume on them—the host was offended. What a disgrace that this rabbi would allow such a woman to touch Him! Yet Jesus rebuked him and pointed out that the three courtesies usually offered a guest had been denied Him. Simon had neglected to give Him water for His feet, to kiss Him, or to anoint His head with oil. It is evident that Jesus valued these Eastern customs. If they had meant nothing to Him, He would not have missed them.

When two angels came to Sodom, Lot observed the courtesies of his time: He rose from his seat, bowed with his face to the earth, and invited them to spend the night at his house and wash their feet. When they accepted the invitation, he baked bread and made a feast. He felt himself responsible for their safety when the men of the city would have attacked them. ". . . do nothing to these men, for they have come under the shelter of my roof."

Peter exhorted Christians to honor all men, honor the emperor. Paul said ". . . outdo one another in showing honor." The great love chapter, 1 Corinthians 13, says "Love has good manners. . . ."

In case Peter and Paul's instructions seem irrelevant to today's carelessly casual styles, we would do well to listen to what a modern philosopher, Eric Hoffer, wrote: "Rudeness is the weak man's imitation of strength."

Courtesy has to become a habit, "a characteristic condition of mind or body, disposition; a thing done often and hence done easily; a tendency to perform in a certain way." Does this sound bad? Is it necessarily hollow just because it's a habit? I don't think so, for if you're in the habit of being courteous, then, even when you're not thinking or feeling rightly, you'll still act rightly; and it's action that counts with other people. It's this you're responsible for before God, not for the vagaries of emotion or mood. What you do to or for others you do to or for the Lord.

Ralph Waldo Emerson said, "'Tis the beginning of civility to make us endurable to each other, to get people washed, clothed, and set up on end."

33

From Silken Self

Several years ago I was asked to give the critique of a modern-poetry reading in a college writers' conference. For an hour or more I listened to what passes nowadays for poetry: dealing with subjects as hunger, terrorism, Vietnam, war, sexism, abortion. A few phrases stick in my mind: mad microbes . . . a world no longer viable . . . the lies of our lives . . . masculine mind-set . . . an armless woman, a blue heron strung up . . . lostness . . . shutting me into the head . . . allowed myself to be cut in two, I was the wrong half . . . power invades all we do . . . the scope of evil too broad . . . journey into self to discover myself and the truth of the life I am living.

The poets assailed us with questions, with condemnation for our collective national guilt and for our personal sins. Almost everything in America was deplored. There was great wailing for our loneliness and our lostness and our hypocrisy. We were examined, dissected, and exhibited, rebuked, attacked, and damned, asked to pity, sympathize, and mourn, to be sensitive, tolerant, and caring. But we were never told how. We were summoned, but to what? There were catchwords, but no touchstone. I listened in vain for some hint that there might be any answer outside of ourselves. The prerequisite for change, according to these (I regret to say) women poets seemed to be a vague journey into the self.

W. H. Auden, asked if he wrote poetry to express himself, said, no, if he had nothing better to express than himself, he would not write poetry.

Most of us in this century take psychology terribly seriously, especially if we know very little about it. While we no longer imagine that we must descend into some Hades or place of dragons in order to know ourselves, we have substituted a journey into the dungeon of our own hearts, where "the deeper the lamp is lowered, the slimier the creatures that are exposed."

That dungeon is not where truth is to be found. Exposing the "creatures" by endless hours of lying on a psychiatrist's couch or letting all one's feelings "hang out" in a sharing group will be not only useless, but will lead to despair, unless the patient is shown a way out of the dungeon.

The exit is away from, not into, ourselves. The summons to be fully a man or fully a woman is the summons to leave ourselves and lose ourselves. No terms could be stronger than those Jesus used: "If anyone comes to me without 'hating' his father and mother and wife and children and brothers and sisters, *and even his own life*, he cannot be a disciple of mine."

These claims were first made vivid to me through the writings of Amy Carmichael of India. She was a true "soldier," having answered the call to service in a very real warfare for the souls of children in India. To read the story of this woman is to forget that femininity has ever meant frivolity and frills. Discipleship holds out the same requirements for both men and women, as Amy Carmichael's prayer so clearly shows:

> From prayer that asks that I may be
> Sheltered from winds that beat on Thee,
> From fearing when I should aspire,
> From faltering when I should climb higher,
> From silken self, O Captain free
> Thy soldier who would follow Thee.
>
> From subtle love of softening things,
> From easy choices, weakenings,
> Not thus are spirits fortified,
> Not this way went the Crucified,
> From all that dims Thy Calvary,
> O Lamb of God, deliver me.
>
> Give me the love that leads the way,
> The faith that nothing can dismay,
> The hope no disappointments tire,
> The passion that will burn like fire,
> Let me not sink to be a clod,
> Make me Thy fuel, Flame of God.

Quotation from *Toward Jerusalem* by Amy Carmichael taken from copyrighted material used by permission of the Christian Literature Crusade, Fort Washington, Pa. 19034.

34

Endurance

While I'm writing this, you are, so far as I know, still single. You are also a Christian. A college-age group in Boston asked me to talk to them about "Sex and the Single Christian." I began my talk by saying that if what they wanted to hear about was sexual *activity* and the single Christian, it would be the shortest speech I'd ever given. The Bible is blunt and rigorous and perfectly clear about this. There is no sexual activity for single people. If you are single, you are committed to sexual abstinence, with no emendations, redactions, or existential expedients. (No ifs, ands, or buts, either!) The steel of manly character is forged in the fires of control and denial.

"You cannot say that our physical body was made for sexual promiscuity; it was made for God, and God is the Answer to our deepest longings."

As you know, Pete, I have been twice widowed, and I know what sexual hunger is, although a woman's is different from a man's, they say—but who in the world can know? It is my experience that God does not remove the physical longing. It is a natural hunger, exacerbated by having been once awakened and satisfied (and Lewis says it is no use knocking on heaven's door for earthly comfort). But it is not by any means the deepest longing of any man or woman, no matter how desperately he or she may insist that it is. Ask any husband or wife who loves his mate if sex perfectly satisfies. It does not. The most passionate couple, who have most assiduously mastered the intricate techniques of *The Compleat Christian Compendium for Coital Contortionists* (don't go looking for that book; it's only a title suggested to me by a well-known theologian!), knows that there is still that "God-shaped vacuum." If, as the Bible says, our bodies are "integral parts of Christ Himself," there is a great deal more than the most perfect and ecstatic human relationship can satisfy.

Don't imagine, Pete, that there is any easy means of sexual control. You've heard all the usual suggestions like cold showers and jogging. They won't fill the bill. Nobody is going to tell you that it's an easy thing to feel the straining of your manhood's powers and restrain them—in single life or in times of abstinence, such as when your wife is ill or in late pregnancy or is just plain tired, or when circumstances deprive you of needed privacy. There's no easy answer, but there is a simple one: endurance. Men who sneer at the word or say, "That's a woman talking!" ignore the fact that Jesus Himself endured, though tempted at every point like any man, and that hundreds of thousands of His followers have, for His sake and by His grace (I repeat: *for His sake* and *by His grace*) also endured. It is cowardly to deny the possibility. Of course it's unusual to endure. It's probably quite extraordinary in this day and age. They will tell you you're some kind of nut. But don't ever let anybody tell you it's impossible. Obedience to God is always possible.

The hope that we Christians have in the Lord Jesus Christ, according to Paul's letter to the Thessalonians, means "sheer dogged endurance." How is a man to endure? Peter gives the answer: "Since Christ had to suffer physically for you, you must fortify yourselves with the same inner attitude that He must have had." It has to begin inside—an utter handing over to the authority of God your whole will and action.

Singleness is a gift, not given to everyone for the whole of life, but given to all for a time. Paul recognized the wisdom of each man having his own wife and each woman her husband, because of the temptation to immorality; but there are those who are "eunuchs." Some of them are born that way, some are made so by others (the practice of castration for various reasons was not uncommon in Jesus' day), and some make themselves eunuchs for the sake of the kingdom of heaven. "He who is able to receive this," said Jesus, "let him receive it." I suppose that Paul was in the last category of "eunuchs." Not that he had literally emasculated himself, but he had accepted the gift of singleness (perhaps he was a widower) in order the better to do the work God had entrusted to him. "To the unmarried and the widows I say that it is well for them to remain single as I do. But if they cannot exercise self-control, they should marry. For it is better to marry than to be aflame with passion."

The great key to that puzzling seventh chapter of 1 Corinthians is the word *call*, or *called*, which occurs eight times in verses 17–24. "Let every one lead the life which the Lord has assigned to him, and in which God has called him."

Married life, widowhood, or single life are valid states in which a Christian may serve God. It is a matter of recognizing His call. (If you read my little book on God's guidance, *A Slow and Certain Light*, you found a few clues as to how a man can recognize the call.)

The willingness to suffer and endure seems to be left out of our training today; even the military is voluntary service, and in order to lure men into it, it is being made less and less demanding. A good soldier is called to endure *hardness*. Hardness is always hard! However, "No temptation has come your way that is too hard for flesh and blood to bear. But God can be trusted not to allow you to suffer any temptation beyond your powers of endurance."

35

Heroes

Of the many young people who tell me that Jim Elliot's life has inspired their lives, it is surprising how many carefully preface their remarks with disclaimers such as, "I don't want you to think I've got him on a pedestal," or, "I don't mean he's a hero or anything."

Well, what is a hero, anyway? "Any man admired for his courage, nobility, or exploits, the central figure in any important event, honored for outstanding qualities." Wasn't Jim a hero? We badly need heroes. How else shall we grasp the meaning of courage or strength or holiness? We need to see such truth made visible in the lives of human beings, and Jim did that, it seems to me.

Tad W. Guzie, S. J., in his book *Jesus and the Eucharist*, says, "We have to go through a process of identifying with heroes and contemplating ideals before we can appropriate ideals and make them our own. This . . . is a basic human truth. There is no way our inner strengths and resources can be tested by the fire of experience unless we have first recognized, through idealization, which strengths and resources make the battle worthwhile."

I was interested to find that the New English Bible uses the word *heroes* in 2 Samuel 23. "These are the names of David's heroes." They were Ishbosheth, Eleazar, and Shammah, "the heroic three," distinguished for courage in battle. Then there were "the heroic thirty," men who had shown courage in one way or another, such as Benaiah, who went down into a pit to kill a lion on a snowy day.

Perhaps we fear the making of such distinctions. I suspect that this fear does not always spring from a sane recognition of the fallibility and sinfulness of all men, but rather, quite simply, from pride. To make a hero of a man is to admit our own shortcomings. This man has done what we've never done and, furthermore, will never do. To put him on a pedestal is to acknowledge his superiority; and, nowadays, that—in the realm of moral courage or purity, as well as in nearly all other realms except sports—is a cardinal sin.

Eric Heiden has just won five gold medals in the Olympics. We don't mind having a hero like that. We admire him for doing what none of us could possibly have done. But to show moral courage or to go into a pit with a lion—that didn't take any special coaching or native physical gifts or slowly acquired skills. In fact (we have to acknowledge, to our shame) *I* might have done it. So we adopt a sour-grapes attitude. We say that we could have done it, but did not choose to. We pride ourselves that we are not plaster saints or goody two-shoes. We even revel in being "sinfuller than thou."

A real man is quick to see what is truly admirable in another. He identifies with him, contemplates what made

139

him what he is, and tries to appropriate the man's methods to reach his own goals.

Heroes are paradigms. They show us what strength or courage or purity actually *looks* like.

Jesus was a hero in a sense. He showed us, in ordinary, everyday terms, what courage looked like. Consider a moment on His last night before the crucifixion. After praying the great prayer of John 17—a prayer for all of us—He had gone with the disciples to the accustomed place, a peaceful garden, where Judas knew he could find Him. Judas arrived with the guard and officers provided by Jesus' archenemies, the chief priests and Pharisees. They came with lanterns and torches and weapons. A man's natural instinct would be to flee or hide.

"Jesus, fully realizing all that was going to happen to him, went forward and said to them, 'Who are you looking for?'" It was a demonstration of quiet courage, born of the knowledge that He was held by the sovereign will of His Father. It was a purely and thoroughly *manly* act.

Jesus was far more than a hero. He was Himself the Way, the Truth, and the Life, "For me to live," Paul said, "*is* Christ. . . ." That truth is radical and transforming.

In his tribute to Mr. Pierson Curtis, former master at Stony Brook School, David Hicks, one of his former students, wrote:

> For many of us "PC" became . . . the absolute authority in our lives that inspired not fear, not awe, not rebellion—but affection. The benevolent despot every boy wants in a father. It was the distance between PC and us boys, because it was the right distance, the just distance, that made us close.
>
> He seldom felt compelled to explain or justify his code to us boys. It was so clear to him, so self-evident that he just lived it without much commentary. . . . There was for him

a right way and a wrong way to do everything, whether to compose a sentence, to set a meal, to address a master, to read a poem, to trim a sail, or to build a fire. PC clung to certain proven, unchanging absolutes of sensible thought and courteous action that in the modern squall of militant and restless change make for dangerous, passionate living. . . . We loved him . . . for his profound acceptance of what we all know to be true, despite our cursed self-centeredness and lazy philosophical relativism: that in life there is a right way and a wrong way, and we must choose the right relentlessly.

I was sitting here, this afternoon, contemplating the current resistance to the idea of heroism, when the phone rang. A publisher friend wanted to know what I thought of a certain manuscript he had sent for my perusal. It was not a very good book, I said, in that it was inaccurate, critical, and missed what I thought was the main meaning of the events it described. But it was well written and well illustrated. It was interesting. It would probably sell rather well, in fact.

"Yeah, that's what I've been thinking," the man said. "We might make a lot of money on that. But of course we're not just in this for the money."

"If you don't publish it, somebody else certainly will."

"That's what I'm afraid of."

"You can be sure of it."

"This business of being a Christian and trying to strike some kind of balance between serving the Lord and making money. I mean you've got to make money to stay in business, and. . . . It drives me crazy!"

"It could mean having to choose, couldn't it? Not striking a balance, but simply losing. Losing money in this case, if you decide it's not a book you ought to handle."

141

"Yeah. Yeah, that's what it could mean."

"But isn't that what Christianity is all about? 'He that loseth his life for My sake shall find it'?"

"Yeah, that's it, all right." Was he thinking, *There she goes with one of those simplistic answers?*

He won't make it into any hall of fame for a decision like that. He might well lose his job. He called weeks later to say they had decided not to publish the book.

Moral choices face all of us, every day. How we choose reveals the stuff we're made of. It is, in the final analysis, the willingness to take the consequences of our decisions that makes heroes: to say, like Luther, "Here I stand. I can do no other."

36

Manliness Means Obedience

When King David was dying, he said to his son Solomon, ". . . Be strong, and show yourself a man, and keep the charge of the Lord your God, walking in his ways and keeping his statutes, his commandments. . . ."

Showing himself a man meant doing what God said. That's what it means today. There will be plenty of opposition. Righteousness has never been popular. You've got to be willing to look like some kind of nut, some of the time, because you won't be doing what everybody else is doing.

There is an idea of masculinity abroad today characterized by the word *macho*. It connotes aggression, ruthlessness, swaggering, even cruelty.

A woman who is about to divorce her husband described him to me as "macho." Nearing forty, he has suddenly adopted a new "image"—full beard, a sea-weedy permanent, designer jeans, chain around the neck. He has bought a high-sprung rough-country vehicle with fat tires and red, white, and blue stripes. He spends a lot of time in sleazy bars, and his wife thinks he has acquired a mistress. One cannot help drawing the conclusion that he is out of touch with reality. It looks as though he does not want to accept his age, his marital status, his image as a descent middle-class businessman, or his responsibilities. He wants "freedom" and "power."

Paul exhorts the Ephesians to conduct themselves "like sensible men, not like simpletons. . . . do not be fools, but try to understand what the will of the Lord is. Do not give way to drunkenness and the dissipation that goes with it, but let the Holy Spirit fill you."

God's man takes the initiative, as he was meant to do, but he is not aggressive. He is strong, but not ruthless; sure, but not swaggering; hard, if need be, but not cruel.

P. T. Forsyth says that hierarchy—the placing of one above another—was meant not for privilege, prerogative, favoritism, or dominion, but for leadership. And leadership means service, sacrifice, help, uplifting, redemption, and a cross. Leadership is not meant to exploit, but to lift; not to exterminate, but to rescue; not to rend, but redeem; not to devour, but to carry; not for primacy, but for priority. It means, in the last analysis, obedience, service, even death, for the sake of others.

The lust for power is as far from the humility of the true leader under God as the lust for sex is from real love. The lusts for power and for sex are characteristic of the man who lives for himself.

144

Make no mistake. If obedience is what marks a man, it can be nothing less than obedience that marks a real woman. The trouble with all of us is that we're disobedient. We're a bunch of "miserable offenders," as the Book of Common Prayer says, "and there is no health in us." Women often ask me what they can do to help men see their responsibility in church and home. The first answer I give is: Be women! If you try to take the responsibilities the man have abdicated, you're not being women, and your disobedience will not help their disobedience. It only adds to the dehumanization of everybody.

Sometimes it looks as though a particular admonition or action would be right, but useless. We turn over and over in our minds whether we should go ahead and try it, but we convince ourselves that there would be no point, "It wouldn't do any good, anyway." That's not always a good criterion. Sometimes obedience means willingness to do the apparently useless thing, in order that God may do the great thing. Do you remember God's calling of Moses? After He had appeared to him in the burning bush, He told him to go to Pharaoh and command him to let the people go, but added that the king of Egypt would not let them go, "unless compelled by a mighty hand." It might have seemed to Moses absurd to deliver a message that would be ignored anyway. If God was going to compel the king, why did He need Moses?

Later on, when the people of Israel were in an utterly impossible situation, with the sea in front of them and the Egyptians pursing them from behind, Moses' faith enabled him to proclaim, "The Lord will fight for you, and you have only to be still." Then God told him to lift up his rod and stretch out his hand over the sea, to divide it, so that the people could go through it on dry ground. Now, if anything would look useless, it would be a gesture like that—to the sea! Yet it was when Moses stretched out his hand that the Lord drove the sea back "by a strong east wind all night."

In the first instance, God could certainly have compelled the king of Egypt without Moses' going down there and speaking to him. In the second instance, God could have dried up the sea by a simple word of command. Why did He need Moses and Moses' faith and Moses' rod and Moses' hand? The answer to that question lies in the mystery of man's will (which is free) and God's will (which is sovereign). God also "needed" the east wind, and the east wind obeyed Him.

I rather imagine that there are times when a woman's determination looks as formidable to a man as Pharaoh's stubbornness and the Egyptian army looked to Moses. His own words, his rod, a gesture like lifting his hand over the sea—how feeble they must have seemed! Yet the power of God was what he counted on. His obedience was a sign of his trust in that unlimited power.

What if a husband, in faithfulness to God and love for his wife, must rebuke her or perhaps speak to her about the relinquishment of something she is determined to hold on to? "What's the point? She'll only be hurt," you say, or, "She wouldn't listen to me, anyway, or she'll get angry. It won't do any *good*." And you back off.

Wait a minute. A woman wants a man who is capable of standing up to her. She wants him to be a godly sort—I didn't say a *pious* sort. That is, she wants him, like Daniel, to have his "windows open," and like Jesus, to have his "face set" toward Jerusalem. If that's the direction he's headed, his obedience will be her liberation.

37

Forgiveness

Recently I listened to a long, sad tale of the wrongs a wife had suffered at the hands of her husband. Since I knew neither of them well, I had no basis for judgment, other than her story, which of course showed him to be a brute and a cad.

"But of course you must forgive him," I said.

"Forgive him? Never."

"Then how will you be forgiven?"

"How will I be forgiven? For what?"

"For your sins."

"What sins?"

"Any of them."

"But I haven't done anything."

"Oh? You haven't sinned?"

"I haven't done anything to him. I've tried my best to work things out. I'm not the guilty one."

I tried to help her to see that she couldn't possibly be without fault in relation to her husband, and when she couldn't see my point, I tried to show her that any sins at all, of whatever kind, could not be forgiven if she refused forgiveness to her husband. If she did not recognize her own need of grace, she could not possibly offer any to him.

Another woman I talked to took the opposite position. She was not denying her own need for forgiveness. She saw herself as guilty—hopelessly guilty, in fact. Her marriage was in a mess, but she had given up expecting any healing. She could talk in a perfectly orthodox way about the theory of salvation by grace, but when it came to the question of her own failures and sins, she could not or would not receive the grace that was there to cover them. Where the first woman did not receive it because she didn't think she needed it, this one did not receive it because she needed more than she thought was available. In both cases, they refused forgiveness to their husbands because they themselves had not accepted forgiveness.

"Forgive us our trespasses as we forgive *those who apologize*" is the way many of us pray the prayer the Lord taught the disciples. Jesus told us to forgive *those who trespass*.

No marriage can survive without forgiveness. Marriage is a long-term, intimate, all-inclusive, no-holds-barred, day-to-day, and year-after-year commitment between two sinners. How will they get along without forgiveness?

A friend who spends many hours each week helping women in trouble in their marriages told me that the first thing she does is to try to help them recognize their own trespasses against their husbands. This is not easy, for they have convinced themselves that it's all his fault. A story that often helps them to see it another way is the one Jesus told Peter when Peter asked how often a man was supposed to forgive his brother. Wouldn't seven times be enough?

No, Jesus said, it would not. Seventy times seven was more like it. Then He told him the story of the king to whom a man owed millions of pounds. The king ordered him to be sold as a slave and his wife and children and everything he had, as well, and the money paid over. At the man's pleading, the king canceled the whole debt, whereupon the debtor went straight out and grabbed by the throat a man who owed him a few shillings. "Pay up!" he said, and when the man begged for mercy, he had him put in prison.

Then his master called him in.

"You wicked servant!" he said. "Didn't I cancel all that debt when you begged me to do so? Oughtn't you to have taken pity on your fellow servant as I, your master, took pity on you?" And his master in anger handed him over to the jailers till he should repay the whole debt.

The truth of the story sinks in, doesn't it? How much more readily our imagination lays hold on reality than does our intellect! We are incensed at the pettiness of the forgiven debtor. Who would behave like that?

Alas. Nobody but us. We are the ones who owe "millions of pounds."

"This is how my heavenly Father will treat you," Jesus said to Peter, "unless you each forgive your brother from your heart." That sin we are so angry about amounts to "a few shillings."

There can be no forgiveness unless there is the acknowledgment that we have been sinned against. Forgiveness is

149

not excusing. To excuse is to make nothing of the sin—to say, for example, he didn't mean to, or he couldn't help it, or he didn't mean it that way. Often this amounts to calling him irresponsible or immature. To forgive is first of all to face the truth: This thing was done to me; this man is responsible; it was wrong. Then it is to treat the person as though the thing were never done and to be willing to be reconciled.

Forgiveness embraces suffering. Saint Francis of Assisi prayed, "Lord, make me an instrument of Thy peace. Where there is injury let me sow pardon."

Sometimes we can be sinned against and not notice it or notice it hardly at all. But there are times when it hurts sharply. There is real injury. It is human nature to want revenge of some sort, even if it is only making sure that the person is aware of having hurt us—and that, I am convinced, is sometimes a form of revenge. It is not human nature to forgive. I have found in my own heart, at times, the sinful lust to see the other person "come crawling."

One who is truly an instrument of God's peace offers, in return for the injury, only one thing: pardon, remembering the millions of pounds he himself owed to the King, and how utterly he was pardoned.

Is there ever a time to talk about the wrong? Yes. Jesus said if your brother wrongs you, go and have it out with him at once. I think that would apply to a wife as well— sometimes. Surely we're not always to go to people who have wronged us, especially if they are not aware of having done so. Often it is better just to forgive in your heart, before God, and perhaps this will give opportunity for the person to recognize his wrong without your prompting, and he will come to you.

"Let there be no more resentment, no more anger or temper, no more violent self-assertiveness, no more slander and no more malicious remarks. Be kind to each other, be understanding. Be as ready to forgive others as God for Christ's sake has forgiven you."

38

Tenderness

There isn't a man or a woman anywhere, I am convinced, who does not long for tenderness. When I was in college, a girl who lived on my floor in the dormitory was pursued by a number of ardent young men on the campus. When the floor phone rang, we assumed it was for her. She was the kind who "could have anybody," it seemed, and treated most of them with casual carelessness. But one young man in particular would not be discouraged in his efforts to win her, even though she kept him at arm's length and declined some of his invitations. She made light of his attentions, as she did of many others', but was given pause one day when a bouquet arrived. Like any woman, she eagerly snatched the card from its tiny envelope. Although one is supposed to be able to "say it with flowers," we all want plain English, too. On the card were two words: *Tenderly, Bill*. I think it did her in. She was a buoyant, outgoing, attractive, sometimes flippant girl, but that word pierced the armor. When she showed it to me, it gave me a whole new vision, through a single powerful word, of what that man was made of. He was not handsome by any means. He was rather ordinary, in fact. But suddenly I saw him as strong and unusually desirable. I had not known that tenderness was an absolutely essential ingredient in a man, but I knew it at once, when I saw the card, and mentally added it to the list of qualifications I would need if I ever found a husband.

Yesterday a woman told me she thought of me as one who always operated on the basis of intellect, instead of emotion. At first it sounded like a nasty crack. I am not sure whether she meant it as a rebuke or a compliment, but in either case it's not true.

If it was sinful emotions she had in mind, then it was a compliment if she thought I never allowed them to influence my behavior. The Bible says we ought not to *act*, for example, from motives of rivalry or jealousy. Feelings are certainly not a very dependable guide for behavior. But if she saw me as a woman never moved by compassion or tenderness, never affected by what others did or said to me, it was not a compliment.

"Christianity is hard as nails," C. S. Lewis wrote. "Hard *and* tender at the same time. It's the blend that does it; neither quality would be any good without the other."

A man must at times be hard as nails: willing to face up to the truth about himself and about the woman he loves, refusing compromise when compromise is wrong. But he must also be tender. No weapon will breach the armor of a woman's resentment like tenderness.

You may not understand her. You may find her unreasonable and illogical and unreachable by any means other than honest tenderness. If she can believe, even for a second or two, that you really want to understand her, that you are earnestly trying to see things from her point of view, she will budge. I know. I'm a woman, and I appear unbudge-able to some, but I also know what a man's arms around me will do to my defenses.

39

Love Is a Refiner's Fire

An old Gospel song describes how we come to Christ:

> Just as I am, without one plea
> But that thy blood was shed for me.

God's invitation is unconditional. We need not, we cannot, meet any prerequisites. We come as we are.

There is a modern song that tells of God's loving me "for just who I am." The lyric implies that God loves everything about us. The shed blood is not mentioned.

Of course God loves us. He is Love. But His love does not stop with just what we are or who we are when we come to Him. He will love us inexorably, changing us into His own image, from glory to glory. How can love be satisfied with any imperfection at all in the beloved?

If a man loves a woman as Christ loved the Church, he is going to do all in his power—he is even going to give his life—to see that she is made holy. He will be tender, but he will also be true. Love is not merely a gentle touch or a pat on the head. It is a *refiner's fire*. It burns to purify.

"What am I supposed to do: put the heat on her?" a man asks. "Start in on every little fault or habit I don't like and make her over again?"

No. You are supposed to do just what Christ did. You have to give yourself. Christ did not come to condemn, but to give His life. It is the Cross that transforms. Jesus gave Himself on the Cross, and there is no power on earth to compare with the power of self-giving. It is a strong weapon against which only pride is a shield. "She is to be free from spots, wrinkles or any other disfigurement—a Church holy and perfect" is what Paul says of the Bride of Christ in Ephesians. That's what Christ wants. That's what any man wants. But how in the world . . . ?

When a man discovers a fault in his wife, it is natural for him to criticize it. If he discovers unfaithfulness, it is natural for him to be outraged, angry, humiliated, and to begin at once to think of ways of getting even. If he follows this "natural" way, he will succeed in making her angry, in digging a huge trench between them, in destroying the ground of communication, and making himself utterly wretched. She will not be purified by this method. The "supernatural" way is: "The husband must give his wife the same sort of love that Christ gave to the Church, when he sacrificed himself for her." It was never Jesus' purpose to "get even."

It seems to me that the first thing a man must do, if he is to purify his wife, is to purify himself, as Jesus had to "sanctify" Himself for us.

"That's a lifetime job," you may say. "So a man can forget about ever getting around to the next job."

It *is* a lifetime job, and he has to work at it ("work out your own salvation with fear and trembling"). But, if he's working at it, aware always of his own need for grace and forgiveness and of the limitations of his own judgment, he will be purifying her, often in ways that he doesn't see.

"The best thing that parents can do for their children, if they want the children to be good, is to be good themselves," someone said. The same goes for husbands who want their wives to be good and holy.

You know that I like things done in an organized way. I'm fussy about many things. I hang sheets on the line outdoors, hems up. I keep kitchen counters nearly bare. I can't stand bric-a-brac. Those things are all in "my department" and don't bother Lars. But, when I try to organize *his* desk and arrange his bookcases, it's another matter. He sometimes thinks it might be a good idea, but not this week, not my way.

He wants me to improve my posture. I've been working on that all my life, with the help of a lot of other people before Lars came along, and I know they were right and he is right. It's still not good enough. When he sees me trying, however, he compliments me. This encourages me to try harder, as no amount of criticizing could do. I guess that's called positive reinforcement.

To sacrifice yourself means to be willing, for one thing, to go through the same refiner's fire you think your wife needs. This takes prayer.

"Search me, O God, and know my heart!" prayed the psalmist. "Try me and know my thoughts!" God will answer that prayer, if it is prayed honestly, and His searching is likely to be painful and surprising. The fault you saw in your wife is likely to show up glaringly in yourself. Your ego is going to suffer. "Try me" is what you ask, and when He answers, you flinch.

157

"See if there be any wicked way in me, and lead me in the way everlasting!" A willingness to acknowledge the "wicked ways" that show up and an earnest request for leading is what God asks of all of us. It does not make us perfect in an instant. It does not exonerate us from future blame. But the man who each day comes to God with this attitude is in a position to "make her holy," as he is commanded to do.

Does it sound preposterous? The demands of Christ often sound preposterous to us sinners. He asks the impossible, as He asked it of the man with the withered hand. He required the one thing the man couldn't possibly do: "Stretch out your hand."

The more Christ-like a man is, the more it will cost him to make his wife the woman she ought to be. He *knows* he's a long way from perfect, and if he ever tries to rebuke or exhort, she will probably remind him of this quite pointedly. Recent sins will provide her with vivid illustrations. It is only human to be cowed by such reminders. We are told in Scripture to consider ourselves before rebuking someone, for we, too, may be tempted to commit the same sin. Yet this does not excuse us from rebuking.

If you come at the business of restoration in a spirit of meekness, you have God's authority to back you up. You wouldn't have chosen this particular responsibility, not in a million years (nor would I have chosen to include this chapter if I hadn't found the subject in the Bible). Criticism, irritation, pickiness, easy condemnation: All of these come only too naturally to most of us and cost nothing to dish out. But a faithful speaking of the truth in love is another thing altogether. A willingness to be refined oneself by that Fire of Love is in a different category. It's what Jesus was willing to do. He went the whole way, obedient even to death, for us.

And when all is said and done, there will be those who will not be moved, who will not heed any rebuke or admonition, no matter how loving. The rich young man "went away sorrowful," and Jesus did not negotiate the terms or pluck at his sleeve. If some would not listen to Him, why should they listen to us?

40

Making Love or Loving

It's one thing to know how to make love. It's quite another to love. You understand by now, I'm sure, Pete, that this book is not one about lovemaking. The bookstores and the racks in airports and drugstores have no shortage of those, but they don't even come close to the subject of real love. It's love I've been talking about: a real man's love for a real woman in the context of the will of God. This is of infinitely greater importance than lovemaking.

I wouldn't want to leave out lovemaking altogether, however. It was God's idea in the very beginning, and He so arranged the world that it was necessary. But he didn't leave it at that. He made it highly pleasurable—even hilarious and fun. "Live joyfully with the wife of thy youth," Solomon said. "Let her breasts satisfy thee at all times." Isaac is described as *sporting* with his wife. The Hebrew word means "playing."

Stern as the Old Testament laws often seem to us to be, there was a humaneness in many of them which may surprise you. Special provision was made, for example, for a man who was newly married: ". . . he shall not go out with the army or be charged with any business; he shall be free at home one year, to be happy with his wife whom he has taken."

Think of that: God wanting young men to be happy and actually issuing a decree to ensure it.

A friend told me that the sum total of her mother's sex instruction to her just before her wedding was, "Never deny your husband. But never say you enjoy it!" Poor woman! She was undoubtedly trying to be very dutiful and very Christian, but what a hideous misconception of God's real design for sex. What a dismal stoicism she took for a substitute. Think of the poor husband! No assurance that she ever enjoyed anything he did, and if her daughter had followed her advice, it could have ruined her marriage.

Sexual intercourse constitutes making yourself one flesh with another person. This is true even if that person is a prostitute. It ought to give us pause. "Avoid sexual looseness like the plague!" Paul said. ". . . Have you forgotten that your body is the temple of the Holy Spirit who lives in you and is God's gift to you, and that you are not the owner of your own body? You have been bought, and at a price! Therefore bring glory to God in your body."

Your body belongs to God not only because He created it, but because He bought it at a high price. It is His right, then, not yours, to give it to a woman. When He does that—when He gives you a wife—then He gives that body of yours to the woman, and he gives her body to you. Take it with thanksgiving! But don't take it selfishly: "The husband should give his wife what is due to her as his wife, and the wife should be as fair to her husband. The wife has no longer full rights over her own person, but shares them with her husband. In the same way the husband shares his personal rights with his wife. Do not cheat each other of normal sexual intercourse. . . ."

Becoming one flesh with the woman God gives you is altogether fitting and proper. God intends for you to abandon yourself and enjoy it. "Live to the hilt every situation you believe to be the will of God," Jim Elliot wrote. I can testify that he did not hesitate to apply the principle to his sex life, the vital condition being the will of God. Until it was the will of God (and you know from his story, *Shadow of the Almighty*, that it took years to be sure) he "pummeled" his body to subdue it, as Paul did.

Sexual experience, so long as it is in obedience and consecration to the Giver of this good gift, will illuminate the truth about Christ and the Church. It's another of those varied physical signs of spiritual facts. It is in losing that we find, in giving that we receive, in dying that we are born. Sex illustrates all three facets of this redemptive truth. If the emphasis in these pages seems too heavy on the giving and the dying, it is because we need it in this era of "be good to yourself" and "have it your way."

Nowhere in our modern world is the radical deterioration of symbols more startlingly seen than in the desanctification of sexuality. People are looking for sex without love, for love without marriage, for marriage without responsibility. The sexual relationship is in fact an epiphany. That means it is the revelation of a reality which is not of this world. Such realities are best understood through symbols, and if we are not faithful in handling those symbols, we lose sight altogether of the reality. Sexuality is a mysterious representation of God's love for us and of the stunning fact of our union with Him. It makes us aware of our limitations as men and women: each dependent upon the other, both dependent upon God for life and meaning and fulfillment, yet marvelously compensated in those limitations by the fact that fulfillment means union. As we share the life of God and enter into His own intimate life and joy, so in the marriage relationship we share each other's lives and enter into the deepest human union where our masculinity and femininity are most gloriously expressed and completed.

I said a moment ago that you ought to *abandon* yourself. There is no better expression of the difference between making love and loving. To make love refers to a performance. It is an act which technically does not require anything remotely resembling real love. To love, by contrast, requires leaving the self behind, abandoning it for the other.

And yet, how shall I write adequately of the rewards of this kind of loving? How, unless you put yourself on the line, can you know that this paradoxical principle really does work?

One of the truths that is often obscured or forgotten by Christians is that the resurrection we look forward to is the resurrection of the *body*. It seems to be taken for granted by many that sexuality will be done away with in heaven. The Bible does not say that. It says there will be no marriage or giving in marriage, and in that respect we will be "like the angels." But it never says we will no longer be sexual beings. We will each have a body. Angels do not have bodies, except in special cases where they were given them in order to perform a special task. Angels are described as "ministering spirits."

Most of what we are told about heaven is quite unimaginable. Even the vivid pictures of the book of the Revelation

163

are too extravagantly fabulous for most of us. The reason we can't grasp the scenes is given us in Romans 8:

> The world of creation cannot as yet see reality, not because it chooses to be blind, but because in God's purpose it has been so limited—yet it has been given hope. And the hope is that in the end the whole of created life will be rescued from the tyranny of change and decay, and have its share in that magnificent liberty which can only belong to the children of God! . . . we . . . are in a state of painful tension, while we wait for the redemption of our *bodies*. . . .

I can't imagine what that redemption of bodies is going to mean, can you, Pete? I simply can't picture it. But I have a hunch that it will be a joy so vast and overwhelming, so all-inclusive and satisfying, that God did not dare to give us more than slight hints, lest we be so distracted by the prospect that we would be unable to do our work. Perhaps, if we bear those hints in mind, love will be not merely something we "make" from time to time, but something we live. Love will be the climate of our homes.

41

Having a Family

Having a family is probably way down on your list of considerations. I doubt if it has even made it to your list of priorities. I don't think I've ever heard of a man getting married in order to have a family—not in our society. I have heard one or two women make that claim.

It is something you will need to think about sometimes, and I strongly recommend that you discuss it with any prospective wife you might happen to come across, be-cause—along with money, in-laws, and sex—it is one of the most potentially explosive issues between husbands and wives.

Some years ago a young couple came to ask my hus-band and me what we thought of their decision not to have children. In a world so full of suffering, with the threat of nuclear war, with overpopulation, they did not see how a

Christian couple could, in good conscience, bring babies into the world.

We told them what we thought: The original intention of intercourse was procreation. God wanted man to propagate himself. For a man and woman of the normal age for begetting and bearing children to enter into marriage without a willingness to have children we believed to be an evasion of the divinely appointed responsibility of marriage. The number of children and the intervals between pregnancies are other questions, but to have or not to have children at all is not an option.

There is a very knotty passage in 1 Timothy about which many pages have been written: women will be "saved through childbearing." Paul can't mean that childless women will all go to hell. Can he mean perhaps that as Christ "saves" His Bride from fruitlessness, so the husband "saves" his wife? In other words since it is our "salvation" to do the will of God, the woman whom God wills to be a mother finds her *salvation*, in that sense, through her husband, "if she maintains a life of faith, love, holiness, and gravity." If, on the other hand, she rebels against the will of God—that is, against the privilege of bearing and rearing children for Him—she will not be living that sort of life. Both husband and wife are "saved" through respecting the divine order.

C. S. Lewis wrote a letter to a couple who, throughout their marriage, had refused to have children, not for the reasons given by our friends, but because they had determined that their lives would be devoted wholly to "us," to the preservation of what seems a perfect love. Lewis wrote:

Begin at the bottom. What wd. the grosser Pagans think? They'd say there was excess in it, that it wd. provoke the

Nemesis of the gods; they wd. "see the red light." Go up one: the finer Pagans wd. blame each withdrawal from the claims of the common humanity as unmanly, uncitizenly, uxorious. If Stoics they wd. say that to try to wrest part of the Whole (US) into a self-sufficing Whole on its own was "contrary to nature." Then come to Christians. They wd. of course agree that man and wife are "one flesh"; they wd. perhaps admit that this was most admirably realised by Jean and you. But surely they wd. add that this One Flesh must not (and in the long run cannot) "live to itself" any more than the single individual. It was not made, any more than he, to be its Own End. It was made for God and (in Him) for its neighbours—first and foremost among them the children it ought to have produced. . . . The experience of a woman denied maternity is one you *did not & could not* share with her. To be denied paternity is different, trivial by comparison.

Those seem strong reasons against choosing to be child-less. As for the argument that the children themselves will have to face suffering, I am tempted to say, "So what else is new?" Suffering is one of the terms of our existence in a fallen world, and if God is sovereign over time and history, He is sovereign over the lives of our children who are, the psalmist says, a "heritage" from the Lord. (I do not write this glibly, believe me. I have grandchildren. What will they have seen and suffered by AD 2030?) The great lesson of faith put to all parents is that of learning to trust God for their children. They love them as they never imagined they could love anyone, and it takes an ever-enlarging faith to believe that God loves them more.

Can you imagine yourself a father? I'm sure you can. Have you ever thought much about your paternal instincts, as such? If you love a woman and find yourself longing to protect her, take her in your arms, and keep her from

167

danger, that's the beginning. There is certainly something of the paternal in a man's love for a woman. But no one can describe to you or prepare you for the actual experience of fatherhood. A letter just came last week from a young man I had known in seminary. His son had just been born. He tried to tell me what an overwhelming experience it was for him. He had had no idea, no idea at all, he said, of how much he was going to love that little baby.

A single man looks with a certain smugness, I suppose, at the harried young couple with the Porta-Crib, the high chair, the potty chair, the kiddie car, the playpen, the diaper bag, and the stuffed toys. Oh, wow! Does it take all that? Is it worth it? Not my scene, man.

Yes, it takes a lot of paraphernalia if you happen to live in civilization. (Indians made do very nicely with one item: a single strip of cloth, about a yard wide and two yards long, which the mother knotted over her shoulder—to carry the baby in, sometimes until he was two years old.) Yes, it takes all that and a whole lot more that you didn't see. But it is worth it, a million times worth it. Not your scene? In the will of God, it will be. And (remember you heard it here!) you will be thankful.

There are plenty of books on fathering. Let me say just one more thing about it here. I am convinced that one of God's reasons for giving us children and animals to care for is to humble us. They begin by breaking our hearts. The total sweetness of a newborn child (or even of a puppy), the innocence, the abject helplessness (here is this person, this small creature who will not survive unless *you* take care of him), the mystery of knowing that this being is the product of your genes and your love (and you see yourself looking back at you out of the milky, wide eyes, the minute he is born): These things will break your heart.

Then, every day, if you take being a father seriously, you'll know that you're not big enough for the job, not by yourself. And that's humbling. The job at the office maybe you can handle. The job of being a husband you might have thought you were doing pretty admirably. Being a son or a brother or a friend or a grandson you probably never gave a whole lot of thought to. But being a father will put you on your knees if nothing else ever did. It will save you from yourself, because you are forced to attend to this very small person for whom you and his mother are responsible. (It is mothers, however, who are even more humbled by their job, simply because usually it is to the mother that the messiest tasks go. "Don't ask me to change the *dirty* diapers," fathers say because they can get out of it. The mother has no choice.)

E. Herman says this about humility:

> We all tend to be infatuated with the idea of strength—but we fail to realize that all true strength is grounded in humility. We still relegate humility to the pale ranks of passive virtues and ornamental graces, whereas, in its legitimate development, it is a stout and soldierly quality. Humility, indeed, is simply a sense of reality and proportion. It is grounded upon a knowledge of the truth about ourselves and about God. "The reason why God is so great a lover of humility," says St. Vincent de Paul, "is because He is the great Lover of truth. Now humility is nothing but truth, whilst pride is nothing but lying."

42

A Checklist

A few of the men in the seminary where I was teaching heard me quote my friend Dorothy, who says, "We're none of us prize packages, dear! Just look for the essentials and skip the rest!" What are the essentials, the men wanted to know, if one is looking for a good wife? They asked me to come and talk to them one evening, so this is what I told them.

At the top of the list would be femininity and faith. She's got to be a real woman, and she's got to be a Christian. No Christian man should consider aligning himself with anybody who lacks those two essentials.

What do I mean by femininity? I've written a whole book about that (*Let Me Be a Woman*, Tyndale), and what I've said in the earlier chapters of the book you're reading now about femininity I'll try to summarize here.

First, she ought to be glad she's a woman. If she's angry or uncertain about her femininity, it usually shows in her dress and manner. It's not hard to tell the difference between the woman who always wears dungarees, backpack, and hiking shoes, whether the occasion calls for it or not, and the woman who wears such garb only when the occasion calls for it, and even then manages, by her bearing and by some little flair, to let you know she's not trying to be a man.

In other words, a real woman has accepted the given: her femininity. This is an act of faith. She accepts the place her femininity gives her in God's world. She knows she was made for man, from man, brought to man by God, and named by him. She does not covet the not given.

A real woman understands that man was created to be the initiator, and she operates on that premise. This is primarily a matter of attitude. I am convinced that the woman who understands and accepts with gladness the difference between masculine and feminine will be, without pretense or self-consciousness, womanly.

A Christian woman acknowledges Christ as her Lord and Master. In so doing, she places herself under obedience, which means that whatever the Lord says to do, she is bound by. Since the Bible says she is meant to adjust, adapt, submit to, and respect her husband, she seeks to do those things *as to the Lord*. This is not the same as doing them purely for the sake of the man. If she is doing it only for him, she will feel justified, whenever he fails, in not adapting and submitting. To be doing it for the Lord changes the picture.

No man wants a zero for a companion. It takes one plus one to make two, not one plus nothing. A woman needs to be clear about this, for only then can she make the rational choice to accept this man as her husband, his name as

171

her name, his destiny as hers, and his faults as part of the condition of this marriage. She is making a choice. She is not at the mercy of some nameless fate, but rather agrees to the proposal of a fallible human being. In order to seal that agreement between them, they stand up in public, "before God and these witnesses," and make their vows. She will not want to delete the word *obey*, for it fits in with the biblical description of what a Christian wife does.

I would certainly include a sense of humor on the checklist. It's essential. I don't mean you have to find a comedienne who will have you rolling on the floor all the time. She doesn't have to be good at telling jokes. But she must know how to laugh—first of all at herself. That's a saving grace.

Dr. James Houston pointed out to me once that the decline of real humor is due perhaps to the loss of congruity. Where there is no congruity, there can be no incongruity, which is the essence of humor. Find a woman who can see the absurd. Flannery O'Connor, one of my favorite twentieth-century writers, was often criticized for creating such grotesque and disagreeable characters in her short stories. "Well," she drawled, in her Georgia way, "I reckon I'm one of the few people left that knows a freak when they see one."

Find somebody who does not take herself so deadly seriously that she has to be always talking about who am I, and how am I relating, and how do I really feel about myself? People who can't laugh at themselves are very hard to live with, because they are doing what Paul says not to do: cherishing exaggerated ideas of themselves and their own importance. Even a glance at the huge gap that yawns between what I ought to be and what I am should suffice to tone down those exaggerated ideas. The discrepancy is, let's admit it, at least absurd. It's said, of course, but it's also laughable.

Now for the question of career. Take a hard look at this one. Any woman you consider for a wife ought to be willing to put her husband and her children first: above her own interests, including a career. This is simple common sense. If she considers a career as important as, or more important than, marriage, don't marry her. That sounds pretty dogmatic, I now; but believe me, trying to mix marriage and a career can be difficult enough. Trying to mix child rearing and a career is impossible. That is not the same as saying that a woman who finds herself suddenly single through widowhood or divorce cannot possibly work to support her children. Hordes of women must and do. But the woman who dreams of doing both, seeing it as an ideal, is in for trouble. She probably cherishes ambitions for herself. She wants to prove that she can do it. She wants to show somebody. There is nothing of God in that wish. Often she feels that she must "serve humanity" by being a doctor or a lawyer or an executive, forgetting that there is no greater service to humanity than the rearing of a Christian family. To seek other avenues, because the home does not seem to be enough or because other avenues look more interesting and promising, is a mistake. If in her mind is the thought of rights—"I have as much right as any man to hold a job"—you are in for trouble. Watch out for the woman who talks of rights!

If she decides to forego or at least postpone a career for the family's sake, here is one place where your wife will greatly need your support and encouragement. She will be an intelligent woman, I am sure, and probably a highly educated one. She will be asked constantly, "What are you doing now?" or, "What are your plans?" To answer, "I'm

Pete's wife," or "I plan to take care of my home and family" will take courage and a calm assurance such as that which sustained Jesus: the assurance that comes from knowing where you came from and where you're going. If you, as her husband, strongly affirm her vocation, it will strengthen her to stand up to the criticism that is bound to come.

Again sacrifice may be called for. There is no getting around the fact that to give yourselves wholeheartedly to the rearing of children for God will eliminate you from a lot of activities your friends are enjoying and often from activities that seem to be obligations—not merely social, but perhaps church, family, business, and civic ones. You will have to ask God for wisdom to choose and the guts to stick to the choice. (Don't pay any attention to you-owe-it-to-yourself talk. You owe nothing to yourself, everything to God.)

William Murchison, in an editorial entitled "Woman as Warrior" in the *Dallas Morning News* (November 27, 1979), referred to General William Westmoreland's pleas before a House Armed Services subcommittee that women not be drafted. With tongue in cheek, Murchison writes, "Only male chauvinist pigs would insult a woman by hinting at her unfitness for helping repel a bayonet charge." He goes on to say:

> The average woman is more important than the average man, important in the sense of holding society together, preventing its dissolution into anarchy.
>
> To mention the word "home" is to excite horror in the breast of the redhot feminist. Home is where simpering little ninnies stay, attending to their tatting. The Real Women are driving trucks or flying B 52s.
>
> But who holds home and family together if not women? . . . It is unfair to assert that her place is in the home; it is absurd

174

to say that the home could exist without her. That is why women are not drafted and sent off to war. With women fighting—and being killed or maimed—the family would suffer a serious blow, and with it, of course, the whole social order.

What reactionary drivel such notions seem to the redhots. Well, too bad. Such notions reflect the thinking of mankind for 6,000 years.

A Canadian reporter accused me of holding to notions about womanhood that were Victorian.

"They're a whole lot older than that," I told her. We only need to go back 2,000 years to find Paul writing to Titus that the younger women should ". . . learn to love their husbands and their children, to be sensible and chaste, home-lovers, kind-hearted and willing to adapt themselves to their husbands—a good advertisement for the Christian faith."

I wonder how many women have gone off to work sometimes more out of greed and a spirit of competition than of necessity, putting little children into day-care centers, simply because there were no strong men behind them to say, "No, you stay home. This is the only job that's really important for you." Other voices were too loud, too alluring, too logical. Yet what a relief the strong man's voice would be.

Look also for "the unfading loveliness of a calm and gentle spirit. . . ." This is Peter's description of the secret of the beauty of holy women.

Recently I had Valerie and her two children—Walter, who is three, and Elisabeth, who is one—visiting me for several weeks. Watching them, I was impressed anew with what a twenty-four hour job mothering is. And how indispensable to the right performance of that job is "a calm and gentle spirit." I saw the Holy Spirit at work in Val, developing that "unfading loveliness."

Look, finally, for a woman who knows that love is not a feeling. It's great if she has lots of loving feelings for you. It's great if she makes you feel loving. Thank God for feelings, for without them we could not respond to all the sensory data in our world. As physical and psychological beings, we are a bundle of feelings. But, as we've already seen, they're no anchor for a marriage. The love that sustains a marriage—and is sustained by marriage itself—has to be action.

My friend Dorothy said, "Skip the rest." It's nice if you find a woman who is beautiful, can cook, loves housework, enjoys the same sports you do, reads your kind of books, and watches your kind of TV shows. If she can sew and sing and ski, pitch a tent, hook up a trailer, build a fire, understand football, balance a checkbook, and clean a carburetor, you'll be an unusually fortunate man. If you're an evening person and she turns out to be the same, be thankful (although, on second thought, I don't know who's going to fix breakfast and get the kids off to school). Be especially thankful if you find a woman who isn't always casting about for heavy topics of conversation. Godliness with contentment is great gain, the Bible says, and so far as I now, neither requires daily intellectual calisthenics.

43

How to Help
with the Checklist

There are five ways you can help that woman who will be
your wife be the woman you want her to be.

First off, be a man. I've said that in a hundred ways,
but I'll say it again. You expect her to be a real woman,
but you can't expect that if you're not a real man. It is in
response to the fullest expression of your manliness that
she will be most womanly. When she's not living up to
your expectations, check yourself out first. Are you taking
the lead as you ought to, with an attitude of humility and
submission to Christ? Are you remembering that you're
the one responsible for her?

Second, make her glad she's a woman. One way to do
this is to notice things. An honest compliment can make her
light up. So she hasn't got the figure of Farrah Fawcett, but

does she carry herself beautifully? Say so. Has she pretty hands? Tell her. Another way is to be courteous. Courtesy is a way of reminding each other that you're a gentleman and a lady. No matter how "old shoe" you both like to be—casual, unstructured, simple, sincere, "just me," or whatever—you'll be surprised what pleasures will unfold if you treat each other with a little special consideration. I've already mentioned some of the specifics: Pull out her chair for her at the table, open a door. Keep on remembering the little things *after* you're married. They often have a way of vanishing, one by one, as familiarity breeds slobbism. Get up some morning, make the coffee, and bring a cup to her in bed, with a daisy or a book on the tray. She'll be amazed.

Lars knows how to make me glad I'm a woman. Gradually and patiently he showed himself a gentleman and made me feel like a lady, during courting days, but the lever that finally tipped the rock was his saying to me one day, "I'm going to be the one building the fences around you, and I'm going to stand on all sides."

Third, understand that leadership is for her help and redemption and be willing to take charge. That includes not making excuses when you fail. It includes spiritual headship in your home. Many men feel that their wives are more spiritually minded, more sensitive to God, more religious, than they are. Therefore they defer to them in the matter of family prayer. They shouldn't. Even if you believe your wife to be your spiritual superior, you are the appointed priest in your home. You need not compete with her. You certainly don't have to preach a sermon at breakfast every morning. Just take the lead in reading a portion of the Bible or the *Daily Light*, that wonderful collection of Scripture verses for morning and evening. Lead in prayer. Let it be as simple as you want, but pray. Ruth Graham said she believes if a husband will pray for his wife and the things she is going to do that day, and if the wife prays for her husband and the things he is going to do, that marriage will be strengthened as the years go by. There is no calculating the influence on the children when their father, by daily example, leads them to God.

Fourth, love her with the love described in 1 Corinthians. Try putting your own name in place of the word *love*: "Pete is slow to lose patience, has good manners, knows no limit to his endurance. . . ." How does it work?

Last, remember that you are heirs together of the grace of life. This is one of the great *equalities* of the Bible, that men and women are all the recipients of the grace that is greater than all our sin. It will cover her sins against you. It will cover your sins against her. It will cover your past and hers. It will cover everything in the future.

In the realm of the operation of grace, distinctions of nationality, social status, and sex are gone. There is no longer Jew and Greek, slave and free man, male and female. And as there is no differentiation between male and female in their both bearing the image of God and in being morally responsible to Him, so there is no differentiation in their being the objects of God's grace. But as they bear the image of the earthly differently (in different physical bodies), so they bear the image of the heavenly differently: the woman in response, the man in initiation.

44

When You Don't Understand Her

One morning last June, when I was staying in a quiet place on Florida's east coast, I went as usual to the long stretch of smooth sand across the road, to watch the coming of dawn. A few stars still shone in the midnight blue, and I walked and prayed, reveling in the cool wind from the sea and the silence.

> Who watched over the birth of the sea,
> when it burst in flood from the womb?—
> when I wrapped it in a blanket of cloud
> and cradled it in fog,
> when I established its bounds,
> fixing its doors and bars in place,
> and said, "Thus far shall you come and no farther,
> and here your surging waves shall halt."

There was a line of shells at the edge of the tide, marking where the surging waves had halted. Seaweed was piled in huge clumps a little higher up, showing that the waves, a few days earlier, had climbed thus far and no farther.

When the edge of the sky began to stain blood red, I sat down on a sand dune to watch the drama of the coming of the sun.

> In all your life have you ever called up the dawn
> or shown the morning its place?
> Have you taught it to grasp the fringes of the earth
> and shake the Dog-star from its place;
> to bring up the horizon in relief as clay under a seal,
> until all things stand out like the folds of a cloak,
> when the light of the Dog-star is dimmed
> and the stars of the Navigator's Line go out one by
> one?

As the stars went out and the bloodstain rose and lightened, filling the eastern sky with pink, I saw that there were towers of thunderheads to the south. White lightning flashed behind them, turning the seas and the edges of the clouds to silver. Behind me in the palmettos I heard the cool, pure notes of the morning dove, interspersed with the cardinal's exuberant whistle. Crabs slid swiftly over the sand, their arched legs seeming to spin like wheels, so that they looked like tiny, delicate royal coaches rushing on some fairy errand.

The sun rose behind clouds, bursting suddenly in a great fan of light, with rays of differing intensity.

Far down the beach, I could see the figure of a man, silhouetted against the bright sea and the bright, set sand. He was bent over, studying something. I knew what it was, for I had studied them myself: the tracks of the great

181

sea turtles that had come out of the sea, during the night's high tide, to lay their eggs in the sand. He was pondering the mystery I had pondered. How did turtles know when the tide had reached its peak? How did they know to dig a deep hole in the dry, warm sand? How did they dig it? (Ever tried digging a deep hole in *dry* sand?)

These mysteries are, Job says, but "edges of His ways." They come from the grand, loving heart of our Creator and Redeemer. I saw them, and I bowed in worship of the Maker of them all, remembering that they, too, will have a part in the mighty song of the Revelation: "Then I heard every created thing in heaven and on earth and under the earth and in the sea, all that is in them, crying: 'Praise and honour, glory and might, to him who sits on the throne and to the Lamb for ever and ever!'"

If, in the will of God, you marry, Pete, I imagine you will find yourself occasionally gazing at this woman who is flesh of your flesh and bone of your bone, awed at the mystery you see there, puzzled, perhaps sometimes infuriated at what seems so mysterious and at times downright irrational in her. Maybe, in the small hours of the night, you will lean on an elbow over her, looking at the sleeping face, at the familiar line of nose, chin, throat, the curve of the breast. Who is she? How was it that she and not another ended up in your life, your house, your bed? What did she mean by what she said at the supper table? Why can't she see what you mean? What is it she wants out of life? Why can't you reason with her? Why doesn't she come straight out and say what she thinks, instead of expecting you to read her mind?

"You husbands should try to understand the wives you live with," Peter wrote in his first epistle, but there is a point beyond which you cannot delve. There are mysteries

God gives you no warrant to plumb. "The glory of God is to keep things hidden." So when you find yourself out of your depth and femininity too fathomless, the words of Thomas a Kempis are worth reviewing:

> Blessed is that simplicity that leaveth the way of hard questions, and goeth in the plain and steadfast way of the commandments of God.
>
> Many have lost their devotion because they would search higher things than pertaineth to them. Faith and a good life are asked of thee, and not the highness of understanding nor the depths of the mysteries of God. If thou may not understand nor grasp such things as be within thee, how mayst thou comprehend those things that be above thee? Submit thyself therefore meekly to God, and submit also thy reason to faith; and the light of knowledge and of true understanding shall be given unto thee as shall be most profitable and necessary for thee.

Do this, Pete, and, with stars and thunderheads, crabs, cardinals, doves, and sea turtles, you, a mere man (but fully a man) may join your voice and sing praise and honor and glory and might to Him who sits on the throne.

Source Notes

Chapter 13

Chapter 14

Chapter 15

Chapter 16

Chapter 19

Chapter 20

Chapter 21

Chapter 22

John 7:17 KJV   86
Genesis 12:1, 4 RSV   86
Jeremiah 1:4–8 RSV   87
Ezekiel 1:3 RSV   87
Romans 1:1 PHILLIPS 87
Genesis 3:12 KJV 88

Chapter 23

1 Corinthians 11:3 PHILLIPS   90
1 Corinthians 11:7 PHILLIPS   90
Ephesians 5:23 PHILLIPS   90
Ephesians 5:25 PHILLIPS   91
Ephesians 5:28 PHILLIPS   91
See Matthew 19:5   91
Ephesians 5:33 PHILLIPS   91
1 Peter 3:7 PHILLIPS   91
1 Corinthians 7:4 PHILLIPS   91
1 Corinthians 11:7 PHILLIPS   91
Ephesians 5:22 PHILLIPS   91
Ephesians 5:24 PHILLIPS   91
Ephesians 5:33 YOUNG CHURCHES   91
1 Timothy 2:12 YOUNG CHURCHES   91
See 1 Peter 3:5   91

Chapter 24

John 6:38; 7:16, 18 PHILLIPS   93
C. S. Lewis, *The Problem of Pain* (N.Y.: Macmillan, 1943), p. 79.   93

Chapter 25

George MacDonald, *Donal Grant*   97
Rolland Hein, ed., *The World of George MacDonald* (Wheaton, Ill.: Harold Shaw, Publishers, 1978), 49.   98
See Hebrews 12:1   98
1 Timothy 4:8 YOUNG CHURCHES   98
1 Timothy 5:21 YOUNG CHURCHES   98

Chapter 26

Genesis 12:1 RSV   99
Genesis 12:5 RSV   99
Daniel 6:3 RSV   100
Daniel 6:23 RSV   100
1 Samuel 18:16 NEB   100
Philippians 2:5–8 YOUNG CHURCHES   101

Chapter 27

1 Corinthians 12:4–7, 27 PHILLIPS   104
Colossians 1:16–18 YOUNG CHURCHES   104
Ephesians 5:23 PHILLIPS, *italics added*   105
Tim Hackler, "Woman Vs. Men: Are They Born Different?" *Mainliner*,
1980.   106
Colossians 3:17 YOUNG CHURCHES   106

Chapter 28

1 Corinthians 9:5 KJV, PHILLIPS   109
Ezekiel 16:8 RSV   111
Hosea 11:4 RSV   111

Chapter 29

John 1:11 PHILLIPS   112
John 15:12 RSV   113
Ephesians 5:25–27 PHILLIPS   113

Chapter 30

Hebrews 2:9 PHILLIPS   117
Hebrews 2:10 YOUNG CHURCHES   118

Chapter 31

1 Corinthians 4:1 PHILLIPS, RSV   121
2 Timothy 2:12 KJV   123
Ephesians 5:28, 29 YOUNG CHURCHES   125
Hebrews 9 YOUNG CHURCHES   125
Hebrews 5:4, 5 YOUNG CHURCHES   125

Chapter 32

See Hebrews 5:1   128
Genesis 19:8 RSV   129
1 Peter 2:17   130
Romans 12:10 RSV   130
1 Corinthians 13:5 PHILLIPS   130

Chapter 33

Luke 14:26 PHILLIPS, *italics added*   132
Amy Carmichael, from *Toward Jerusalem* (London: Society for Promoting
Christian Knowledge, 1936), p. 94.   133

Chapter 34

1 Corinthians 6:13 YOUNG CHURCHES   134
1 Thessalonians 1:3 PHILLIPS   136
1 Peter 4:1: YOUNG CHURCHES   136
Matthew 19:12 RSV   136
1 Corinthians 7:8, 9 RSV   136
1 Corinthians 7:17 RSV   136
1 Corinthians 10:13 PHILLIPS   137

Chapter 35

John 18:4 PHILLIPS   140
Philippians 1:21 KJV, *italics added*   140

Chapter 36

1 Kings 2:2, 3 RSV   143
Ephesians 5:15, 17, 18 NEB   144
Exodus 3:19 RSV   145
Exodus 14:14 RSV   145
Exodus 14:21 RSV   146

Chapter 37

Matthew 18:15   149
Ephesians 4:32 YOUNG CHURCHES   151

Chapter 39

"Just As I Am" by Charlotte Elliott   155
Ephesians 5:27 PHILLIPS   156
Ephesians 5:25 PHILLIPS   156
Psalms 139:23 RSV   157
Psalms 139:24 KJV   158
See Luke 18:23   159

Chapter 40

Genesis 26:8 KJV   160
Deuteronomy 24:5 RSV   161
1 Corinthians 6:18–20 PHILLIPS   161
1 Corinthians 7:3–5 PHILLIPS   161
1 Corinthians 9:27 RSV   162
Romans 8:20, 21, 23 PHILLIPS, *italics added*   164

Chapter 41

See 1 Timothy 2:15   166

Sheldon Vanauken, *A Severe Mercy* (N.Y.: Harper & Row, 1977), p. 207.　166
E. Herman, *Creative Prayer* (Cincinnati, Ohio: Forward Movement Publications, n.d.), pp. 13, 14.　169

Chapter 42

Titus 2:4, 5 Phillips　175
1 Peter 3:4 Phillips　175

Chapter 44

Job 38:8–11 NEB　180
Job 38:12–15 NEB　181
Revelation 5:13 NEB　182
Thomas a Kempis, *The Imitation of Christ*, 4. 18.　183

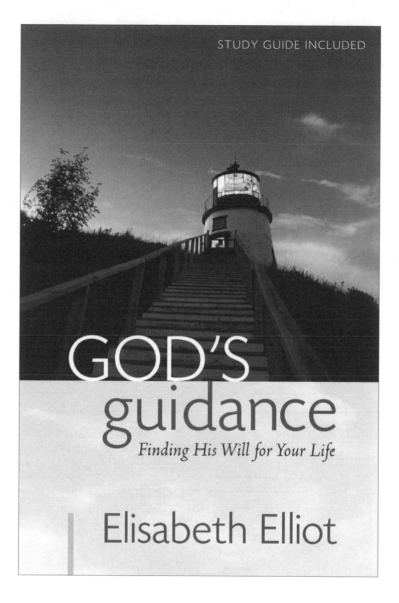

STUDY GUIDE INCLUDED

GOD'S
guidance
Finding His Will for Your Life

Elisabeth Elliot

Respected author invites readers
to draw closer to God

The Journals of

JIM ELLIOT

At 21, he began an adventure that would require
the ultimate sacrifice.

EDITED BY

ELISABETH ELLIOT

The author of *Through Gates of Splendor*

An amazing story of
courage and determination